MAYER SMITH

A Kingdom Stolen by Love and Blood

Contents

One

The Heist That Changed Everything

T he night was thick with shadows, the air cloying with the scent of damp stone and rotting wood. A quiet drizzle misted the rooftops of Whitecliff, its sleek towers standing as pale sentinels against the black sky. The city slept, unaware that within its grandest estate, a thief moved unseen.

Silence was her oldest companion. Shadows, her closest ally.

Kaela pressed her back against the cold wall, heart steady, breath measured. The nobleman's manor loomed before her, perched atop the city like a king watching over his dominion. She had studied its defenses for weeks—the patrolling guards, the locked windows, the servant's entrance where careless hands sometimes left latches undone. But none of it compared to the prize within.

The Bloodstone.

A jewel as red as spilled life, large enough to buy her way out of the underbelly of Whitecliff and into a future where no lord's blade would ever find her back. A future where she was more than a whispered name in the streets, more than a girl who lived on stolen coins and broken promises.

She counted her breaths. One. Two. Three. Then, she moved.

Slipping through the open servant's entrance, she darted down a narrow corridor, her soft boots making no sound on the stone floor. A faint glow of candlelight flickered from a room down the hall, the sound of a yawning servant carrying through the space. She pressed herself against the wooden frame of a doorway, waiting.

Footsteps. A pause. A sigh. Then, the door shut, and the servant retreated up the stairs.

Kaela wasted no time. She took the path she had memorized, weaving through the lavish halls, past thickly woven tapestries and silver-trimmed candle holders. The nobleman was away, attending some grand feast, and most of the guards were stationed outside, never suspecting that the true danger lurked within.

The vault was behind a heavy door reinforced with iron bars, an elaborate lock sealing it tight. Any ordinary thief would have turned back. Kaela was no ordinary thief.

She crouched, pulling two slender pins from the leather strap on her wrist. In the quiet, she could hear the lock's mechanism like the beat of a drum. She worked quickly, feeling for each tumbling pin within the keyhole, counting the seconds before someone might walk past.

Click.

The lock gave way, the door creaking open just enough for her to slip through. Inside, the vault smelled of dust and old parchment, shelves stacked with scrolls and ledgers, golden trinkets forgotten in their corners. But her eyes found only one thing—the pedestal at the center of the room, where the Bloodstone sat beneath a thin glass dome.

Her fingers itched as she stepped closer, breath shallow, the thrill of the steal making her pulse quicken. She reached into her pouch, pulling free a folded cloth, ready to lift the gem and wrap it safely away.

That was when she heard it.

A breath.

A shift in the darkness.

Her instincts screamed at her, but she was too late. A hand clamped over her wrist, another at her throat.

Kaela twisted, dropping low and kicking out. Her attacker staggered, but not for long. He was quick—quicker than any nobleman's guard had a right to be. She felt the sharp press of steel against her ribs before she could regain her footing.

"Who sent you?" The voice was low, edged with authority.

Kaela's mind raced. She could barely make out his face in the dim glow of the lanterns lining the corridor, but his grip was strong, practiced. He wasn't just a guard.

She swallowed down the panic. She had been in worse situations before.

"No one sent me," she said evenly. "I work alone."

A pause. Then, the blade eased from her ribs.

"You shouldn't be here."

She almost laughed. "Neither should you."

For the first time, she caught a glimpse of his face. His hood had slipped slightly, revealing dark hair, sharp cheekbones, and something she hadn't expected. A noble's bearing. A prince's arrogance.

Realization slammed into her. She had seen that face before. Not in person, but in the worn paintings that still hung in Whitecliff's halls.

The lost prince.

Kaela's grip on her dagger tightened.

"You're supposed to be dead."

His eyes narrowed. "And yet, here I stand."

Her mind raced through the possibilities. The lost Prince Raelan, heir to the throne of Whitecliff, had been missing for nearly a decade. Killed in the coup that had placed his uncle on the throne—or so the story went. Yet, here he was, very much alive, standing between her and her freedom.

"You have one chance," he said. "You can put that dagger away and hear me out, or we can see who's faster with a blade."

Kaela measured him, measured the weight of her choices. She could run. She could fight. But something about his gaze told her he would not go down easily.

"I don't make deals," she said.

He smirked. "You just haven't been offered the right one."

She hesitated. She hated hesitating.

Then, from the hall beyond, the sound of approaching footsteps shattered the fragile moment.

Guards.

Raelan's expression darkened. He grabbed her wrist before she could retreat. "If you want to live, you'll follow me."

Kaela had spent her entire life trusting no one but herself. But for the first time, she wasn't sure if she had a choice.

The voices grew closer, metal armor clinking in the silence.

She gritted her teeth.

"Damn you, prince."

Then, together, they ran.

Two

A Fugitive's Fate

Rain lashed against the stone walls of Whitecliff as Kaela sprinted through the narrow alleyway, her breath coming in sharp, measured bursts. Behind her, the clatter of armored boots echoed against the cobblestone streets, the guards shouting orders into the night.

"Find them! Block the southern gates!"

Her fingers tightened around the wrist of the man running beside her—the prince, the supposed ghost of a dead heir. Raelan kept pace with her, his grip firm as they twisted through the maze of backstreets and abandoned corridors of the old quarter.

She should have left him behind. She should have chosen herself, as she always had. But there had been something in his eyes back in that vault—something dangerous, something desperate. And Kaela had spent enough time surviving to recognize when someone had everything to lose.

A sharp whistle split the air. The signal of a scout spotting their movement.

Kaela cursed under her breath. "We need to get off the streets."

"Where?" Raelan demanded, his voice steady despite the chase.

Kaela yanked him into a side street, pressing her back against the damp stone as a patrol rushed past the main road just ahead. Water dripped from the overhanging rooftops, mixing with the sweat on her brow. She barely had a second to think before another sound cut through the storm—horses.

"They're bringing the cavalry?" Raelan whispered.

"That means they won't stop searching anytime soon," Kaela muttered. "They must have recognized you."

A flicker of something crossed his face. "Good."

She shot him a look. "Good? Are you mad?"

"They'll know I'm alive." His voice was tight, controlled. "That means my uncle will know. And that means he'll start making mistakes."

Kaela inhaled sharply. He wasn't just some lost prince crawling out of the shadows. He had a plan. And that made him even more dangerous than she thought.

Footsteps neared again. This time, she had seconds to act. Without warning, she grabbed Raelan by the collar and shoved him backward. His back hit the door of an abandoned shop with a muffled thud.

"Hey—"

"Shut up."

She reached into her belt, pulled free a slim metal pick, and jammed it into the rusted lock. The storm masked her movements, but she knew they were cutting it close. Voices carried over the wind, guards barking orders.

Click.

The door swung inward.

She shoved Raelan inside first, slipping in behind him just as a torchlight flared outside.

The moment the door shut, the room was swallowed in darkness.

Kaela pressed her back against the wall, barely breathing. Outside, the glow of the torches flickered through cracks in the wooden planks covering the windows.

"Check this street!"

Raelan shifted beside her. "They'll—"

She pressed a hand over his mouth, her body taut against his. His breath was warm against her palm, his heartbeat steady under her fingertips. The silence between them stretched, thick with tension.

Then, a boot kicked at the door.

Kaela froze.

Another.

She forced herself to remain still, ignoring the way her pulse pounded in her throat. The guards muttered among themselves, something about splitting up.

Another kick.

The wood groaned but held.

Kaela bit the inside of her cheek. If they forced their way in, they'd have no escape. Her daggers would do little against a trained patrol, and the prince—what skills he had, she had yet to see.

The sound of a horse snorting nearby caught the guards' attention.

"Move along! They wouldn't have made it this far without being seen."

The boots retreated.

Kaela didn't dare exhale until their voices had faded completely.

Only then did she release her grip, stepping back from Raelan.

"You're a reckless fool," she whispered.

He let out a slow breath, his features barely visible in the dim light. "And you're a skilled thief."

She turned away from him, running a hand through her damp hair. They couldn't stay here. The shop was abandoned, but it wouldn't remain unnoticed forever.

"We need to get to the lower quarter," she murmured.

Raelan frowned. "Why?"

"Because the noble streets belong to your uncle, and the lower quarter belongs to me."

For a second, he hesitated. Then, he nodded.

Kaela moved first, stepping carefully around the ruined shelves and shattered glass littering the floor. A draft snaked through the cracks in the walls, carrying the scent of mildew and old parchment. She pushed open the back door, peering into the dark alley beyond.

Clear.

She turned back to him. "Follow me."

They slipped into the night, avoiding main roads, moving like ghosts through the slums of Whitecliff. Here, the houses leaned together as if they were too tired to stand on their own. The streets were thick with the smell of burning tallow and unwashed bodies. But these alleys held safety in a way the grand estates never could.

Kaela led them through a twisting route until they reached a battered wooden hatch at the end of an alley. Without hesitation, she knelt, pulling up the concealed door to reveal a stone tunnel beneath.

"You've had a hiding place this whole time?" Raelan asked, raising an eyebrow.

"Not a hiding place," she corrected. "A way out."

She slipped down first, the cold dampness of the tunnel wrapping around her like a second skin. She had built this escape long ago, brick by stolen brick. A tunnel that led beneath the city walls—an exit for when Whitecliff became too dangerous to survive.

Raelan followed, shutting the hatch above them. Darkness swallowed them whole.

Kaela moved forward without hesitation. "Stay close," she whispered. "Step where I step."

They moved in silence, the tunnel stretching ahead, the sound of dripping water echoing around them. Minutes passed, but she didn't stop. Not until she reached the far end where the tunnel sloped upward.

Another door. Another lock.

She made quick work of it, pushing open the exit that led outside the walls.

Cold night air hit her lungs as she stepped out into the open.

Raelan followed, exhaling sharply as he looked back toward the city. "We're out."

"For now," she murmured.

They weren't safe yet. They had bought themselves time, nothing more.

Raelan turned to her, his gaze sharp. "We need to talk."

She crossed her arms. "About what?"

"You saved my life tonight."

Kaela snorted. "Not by choice."

His lips curved slightly. "Perhaps not. But you did. And now I need something more from you."

She stiffened. "I'm not a hero, prince."

"No. You're not," he agreed. "You're a thief. And I need a thief."

Kaela felt her stomach twist. She had spent her whole life running from the grips of noblemen, from the weight of their demands. She had never wanted to be part of anything but her own survival.

And yet, standing there in the night, beneath a sky filled with rain and the taste of escape on her tongue, she knew she was already too deep in this.

"What do you want?" she asked, voice steady.

Raelan held her gaze.

"I want my kingdom back."

Three

A Kingdom in Chains

The rain had stopped by dawn, leaving the world shrouded in damp mist. From their hidden perch atop the old ruins beyond the city walls, Kaela could see Whitecliff stretched before them like a slumbering beast. The high spires of the castle pierced the sky, their pale stone catching the first hints of daylight. The city, despite the hour, was already stirring with life.

Kaela pulled her cloak tighter around herself, shivering against the morning cold. She had spent years navigating those streets, knowing every hidden passage, every unwatched alley. But looking at it now, through the eyes of a fugitive, it felt like an entirely different world.

She felt Raelan's presence beside her before he spoke.

"You see it, don't you?" His voice was quiet, but there was a sharp edge beneath the calm.

Kaela didn't answer at first. She studied the city—the castle gates lined with armored guards, the banners bearing the sigil of a golden wolf against crimson. Not his family's sigil, but his uncle's.

"I see it," she muttered.

"A kingdom in chains," Raelan said, his jaw tightening. "They may not realize it, but my people are prisoners."

Kaela arched a brow. "I see plenty of free men walking about."

Raelan turned to her then, his dark eyes burning. "Freedom isn't just about walking through a city, Kaela. It's about knowing you own your fate. My uncle has spent years tightening his grip on Whitecliff. He's rewritten laws, silenced dissenters, and bled the people with heavy taxes to fuel his war machine."

Kaela folded her arms. "War machine?"

"He's raising an army," Raelan said. "Not just to secure his rule, but to expand it. The kingdom to the north—Elderran—they're on the brink of collapse. If my uncle moves quickly, he can seize their lands before their new king even has a chance to rally."

Kaela's gaze flickered back to the city. She'd spent so long worrying about her next job, her next meal, that she had never considered the grand game being played above her. But now, she was standing next to the man who had once been meant to wear the crown.

And he wanted it back.

"What exactly do you need me for?" she asked.

Raelan studied her for a long moment before speaking. "I need to know what my uncle is planning. His army, his strategies—if I'm going to take back my kingdom, I need information."

Kaela let out a low laugh. "You want me to spy on the most powerful man in Whitecliff? You do realize that if I get caught, I'll be lucky if he just kills me."

Raelan's expression didn't change. "I do."

"Then why should I risk my neck?"

He stepped closer. "Because I can offer you something no one else can."

Kaela arched a brow. "And what's that?"

Raelan's lips curved, but there was no humor in his smile. "A future."

Kaela's stomach twisted. He was a noble, a prince, a man who had once been raised to rule. He didn't understand that people like her didn't have the luxury of futures. They had only the present, only survival.

And yet…

She turned away, exhaling sharply. "Say I agree. How do I even get close to your uncle?"

"I have a contact inside the castle," Raelan said. "Someone who's been waiting for my return."

Kaela's fingers twitched at her sides. Getting into the castle was one thing. Getting out? Another problem entirely.

"Who's this contact?" she asked.

Raelan hesitated. "Someone I trust."

"That's not an answer, prince."

He let out a slow breath. "Captain Aldric."

Kaela's blood went cold. "Aldric?" she repeated. "You mean the King's Hound?"

The man was a legend in the underworld of Whitecliff. A soldier turned executioner, loyal only to the throne. Rumors said he had no mercy, that his blade never hesitated. He had hunted down rebels, thieves, and traitors alike, all in service to the crown.

And Raelan expected her to trust him?

"You've lost your mind," she said flatly.

Raelan met her gaze. "He served my father before he was forced to swear allegiance to my uncle. If there's anyone in the castle who still believes in my family's rule, it's him."

Kaela shook her head. "Or maybe he's been loyal to your uncle for so long that he'll turn you in the second he sees you."

Raelan's jaw clenched. "It's a risk I'm willing to take."

Kaela sighed. "Of course you are. It's not your head on the chopping block if this goes wrong."

Raelan smirked. "No, but it's my throne."

She hated how easily he spoke about reclaiming something that had been lost for a decade, as if it were as simple as walking through the front gates and taking a seat. But as much as she wanted to turn away, to forget this entire conversation, she couldn't.

Because if Raelan was right—if Whitecliff was truly preparing for war—then there was no place left for someone like her.

And maybe, just maybe, she wanted to see if he could actually pull this off.

She let out a long breath. "Fine. I'll get into the castle. I'll find Aldric."

Raelan's expression didn't change, but she saw something flicker in his eyes—relief.

"But if this goes wrong," she warned, "don't expect me to come back for you."

"I wouldn't dream of it."

She turned away, shaking her head. "Damn fool prince."

And with that, she disappeared into the morning mist, ready to step into the lion's den.

Four

A Deal in the Dark

The city was alive with whispers.

Kaela moved through the twisting alleys of Whitecliff, her steps careful, measured, as she kept to the shadows. The scent of damp stone and gutter smoke filled the air, masking her presence. The nobility feasted in their grand halls, drowning themselves in wine, while the slums stirred with unrest. Word of tightened patrols spread like wildfire, murmurs of the fugitive prince slipping between lips like secrets meant to be kept.

If Raelan had hoped to go unnoticed, he had failed.

Kaela adjusted her hood, pulling it lower as she neared the edge of the market district. It was quieter here at night, the rows of abandoned stalls lining the streets like sentries standing watch. But it was not the markets she sought. It was the tunnels beneath them.

The entrance was exactly where she remembered. A half-rotted wooden grate behind the old butcher's stall. She crouched, her fingers prying it open just enough to slip inside. The scent of damp earth and mold rushed to meet her.

She descended.

The tunnels were remnants of a forgotten age, a labyrinth carved beneath Whitecliff long before the city's golden age. Few remembered them, and even fewer dared to enter. Those who did were either desperate or foolish.

Kaela was both.

Her footsteps barely made a sound against the slick stone as she navigated the narrow passageway. Water dripped from above, a steady rhythm that filled the silence. She kept one hand near her dagger, the other brushing against the wall as she moved forward.

A few twists. A few turns. Then she saw it.

A flickering light in the distance.

She slowed her steps, every muscle tensed. The tunnels were not empty. They never were.

As she approached, she caught the scent of burning oil. A

lantern, set upon a crate in the center of the open cavern ahead. And beside it, seated upon another crate, was the man she had come to find.

Captain Aldric.

The King's Hound.

He looked up as she stepped into the glow of the lantern, his sharp eyes cutting through the dim light. His dark leathers were worn, but his armor was well-kept, his sword resting easily against his knee.

Kaela had heard stories of him since she was a child. Some said he had killed a hundred men in the king's service. Others claimed he had once let a traitor escape, only to hunt him down a year later, when the man had begun to believe himself safe.

A hunter who never stopped hunting.

She had spent her life avoiding men like him.

Kaela took a slow breath, then pulled back her hood.

"Aldric," she said, keeping her voice neutral.

His gaze didn't waver. "Kaela. It's been a long time."

She had met him once before, years ago, when she had been nothing more than a street rat trying to steal from the wrong noble's pocket. He had let her go with only a warning. A mercy she had never quite understood.

She didn't expect him to offer it again.

"I assume you know why I'm here," she said.

Aldric leaned forward slightly, resting his forearms against his knees. "I know you've been seen with a man who should not be alive."

Her heartbeat slowed. He was testing her.

"And what if I have?" she asked.

Aldric studied her for a long moment. Then, he sighed.

"You wouldn't be here if you didn't believe in him."

Kaela almost laughed. "Believe in him? I don't believe in anyone."

Aldric smirked, but there was no warmth in it. "That's a shame. Because if you're here, it means you're already caught up in something you can't walk away from."

She hated that he was right.

Kaela crossed her arms. "Raelan said you were once loyal to his father. That you still might be loyal to him."

Aldric didn't speak right away. He reached for the lantern,

adjusting the wick, the light flickering against the damp stone.

"When the king was murdered," he said, his voice low, "I swore my allegiance to the crown. Not to the man who wears it, but to the throne itself." He lifted his gaze. "That throne belongs to Raelan."

Kaela frowned. "Then why are you still serving his uncle?"

Aldric let out a breath. "Because loyalty doesn't always mean open rebellion. Sometimes, it means waiting. Watching. Choosing the right moment."

Kaela narrowed her eyes. "And what? You think this is the right moment?"

Aldric didn't answer right away. He studied her instead, as if weighing something in his mind. Then, he shifted, pulling something from beneath his cloak and tossing it toward her.

She caught it instinctively, her fingers curling around cold metal.

A key.

She looked up.

"The records chamber beneath the castle," Aldric said. "Inside, you'll find the names of every man currently enlisted in the royal guard, as well as the supply routes for the coming months." He paused. "If Raelan wants to take back his throne, he'll need to know who his enemies are—and who might be willing to betray them."

Kaela turned the key over in her palm. "You're asking me to break into the castle."

Aldric smiled faintly. "I'm not asking you anything. I'm simply leaving you with a choice."

Kaela exhaled slowly. "And what happens if I take this key and never return?"

Aldric leaned back. "Then I'll assume you're dead."

She stared at him. "You're really willing to risk everything for him?"

Aldric's expression didn't change. "I've already risked everything. Now I intend to finish what I started."

Kaela's grip tightened around the key.

She hated this. Hated being pulled into something larger than herself. But at the same time, she knew the truth.

There was no going back now.

She shoved the key into her belt, adjusting her cloak. "You better pray you're right about him."

Aldric's lips curved slightly. "You'll find that faith can be a powerful thing, Kaela."

She snorted. "I don't have faith."

Aldric smirked. "Then I suppose we'll have to rely on skill instead."

Kaela turned without another word, slipping back into the shadows of the tunnel.

She could feel the weight of the key against her hip as she moved.

A key that could change the fate of a kingdom.

A deal made in the dark.

And a choice she could no longer run from.

Five

The Web of Betrayal

The rain had returned by the time Kaela emerged from the tunnels. It dripped from the rooftops, slithered down her cloak, and seeped into her boots. She hated the way Whitecliff smelled after a storm—like wet stone and decay. The city had always been rotting, its filth hidden beneath the polished grandeur of the noble districts.

Tonight, though, it wasn't just the city that felt like it was festering.

The key Aldric had given her felt heavy in her pocket, pressing against her side like a brand. She should have thrown it into the harbor, let it sink to the bottom and be forgotten. But she hadn't.

Because some foolish part of her, some reckless part, wanted to see this through.

Her fingers tightened around the edge of her cloak as she moved through the winding streets of the lower quarter. The castle loomed in the distance, its towers reaching toward the sky like skeletal fingers. Somewhere inside, behind its thick stone walls, lay the records Aldric wanted—the names of those who served the false king, the paths of the supply routes that fueled his growing army.

And if Kaela was going to get to them, she needed a plan.

She slipped through the familiar maze of back alleys until she reached the Flickering Lantern. A tavern nestled against the crumbling remnants of an old watchtower, its roof sagging, its door hanging slightly off its hinges. It didn't look like much, but it was one of the few places in Whitecliff where coin spoke louder than loyalty.

Inside, the air was thick with the scent of ale and damp wood. The room was crowded with sailors, mercenaries, and thieves, all speaking in hushed tones over their drinks. Kaela moved through them without drawing attention, her steps light, her hands ready.

She spotted him in the corner, sitting alone at a table near the fire.

Orin Locke.

He was a smuggler, a forger, and, more importantly, the only man in Whitecliff who knew how to get into the castle without being seen.

Kaela slid into the seat across from him.

Orin didn't look up. He simply lifted his tankard to his lips and took a slow sip before speaking.

"If you've come for a favor, Kaela, I suggest you leave while you still have your fingers."

Kaela smirked. "That's not very welcoming."

He set his drink down, finally meeting her gaze. His face was sharper than she remembered, the lines around his mouth deeper. The years had hardened him.

Orin let out a low sigh. "What do you need?"

She leaned in slightly. "A way into the castle."

His expression didn't change, but she saw the flicker of something in his eyes—caution, maybe even a touch of amusement.

"You've lost your damn mind," he muttered.

Kaela shrugged. "Wouldn't be the first time."

Orin exhaled slowly, rubbing a hand over his face. "I don't know what you're tangled up in, but breaking into the castle? That's not the kind of trouble you walk away from."

She slid a small pouch across the table. It landed with a dull clink.

Orin raised an eyebrow but didn't reach for it.

Kaela's voice was low when she spoke. "There's more if you help me."

He studied her for a moment, then let out a bitter chuckle. "You always did have a death wish."

Kaela smirked. "So, will you help me or not?"

Orin leaned back in his chair, his fingers tapping against the wooden table. "There's a passage beneath the eastern tower. Old, forgotten by most. But it won't be unguarded."

She nodded. "I can handle that."

Orin shook his head. "No, you don't get it. The guards there aren't just men with swords. They're trained hunters. The kind who don't ask questions before putting a knife in your ribs."

Kaela's stomach tightened. "That's my problem, not yours."

Orin sighed. "You're serious about this, aren't you?"

She didn't answer.

He muttered a curse under his breath. "Fine. But if you get caught, don't you dare breathe my name."

She smirked. "Wouldn't dream of it."

Orin reached into his coat and pulled out a scrap of parchment. "This is the route you'll take. There's a small window of time before the next patrol. If you miss it, you're dead."

Kaela took the parchment, her fingers brushing against his. "You have my thanks."

Orin snorted. "Keep it. You'll need it more than me."

Kaela didn't linger. She slipped out of the tavern, stepping back into the cold night air.

The castle awaited.

—-

The passage was exactly where Orin said it would be—a narrow crevice hidden behind the remnants of an old supply house. The entrance was blocked by a rusted iron grate, but Kaela made quick work of the lock, slipping inside without hesitation.

The air was thick with dampness. The tunnel sloped downward, its walls slick with moss and grime. She moved carefully, her footsteps silent against the stone.

Minutes passed.

Then she saw them.

Guards.

Two men, standing at the far end of the tunnel, their torches casting long shadows against the walls.

Kaela pressed herself against the stone, watching. She had seconds to act before they turned.

She drew her dagger, moving swiftly.

The first guard barely had time to register her presence before her blade found his throat. He let out a choked gasp before crumpling to the ground.

The second turned, reaching for his sword—

Kaela was faster.

She drove her dagger up beneath his ribs, twisting hard. The man let out a strangled groan before slumping against her, his weight heavy, his blood warm against her hands.

She exhaled, stepping back.

The way was clear.

She continued forward, her heartbeat steady, the castle looming above her.

She had made it inside.

Now came the hard part.

—-

The records chamber was deep within the castle, hidden behind layers of locked doors and guarded halls. But Kaela had studied its layout.

She moved swiftly, avoiding the main corridors, slipping through the servant passages where few would look twice at a shadow in the dark.

Finally, she reached the chamber.

The door was heavy, reinforced with iron. But the lock—

Kaela pulled out the key Aldric had given her, sliding it into place.

Click.

She slipped inside.

Rows of shelves stretched before her, stacked high with scrolls and ledgers. She moved quickly, scanning the markings, searching for what she needed.

Then—

A name.

She froze.

One of the ledgers was marked with the names of those who had sworn fealty to the king.

She ran her fingers down the list.

And there, at the bottom—

Captain Aldric.

Her blood turned to ice.

The door behind her creaked open.

She spun, her dagger already in her hand.

Aldric stood in the doorway, his expression unreadable.

Kaela's heart pounded. "You lied to me."

Aldric sighed. "Not entirely."

Her grip tightened on the dagger. "You swore fealty to the king. You were never waiting for Raelan. You were waiting for me."

Aldric stepped forward, his eyes cold.

"I told you, Kaela," he murmured. "Loyalty doesn't always mean rebellion."

Then the guards stormed in.

Six

The Prince's Betrothal

Pain.

Kaela's head throbbed as she stirred, her limbs heavy, her wrists aching from the rough iron shackles biting into her skin. The world around her swayed in shadowed blurs, the damp scent of stone and old blood filling her nostrils. The cold seeped into her bones, and for a brief, terrifying moment, she thought she had woken in a grave.

Then she heard footsteps.

Her senses sharpened. Chains rattled as she moved, her fingers brushing against the rough stone floor. Her weapons were gone. Her hood, her daggers, even the small lockpick she kept sewn inside her sleeve—all stripped from her.

"Awake at last," a voice drawled from the darkness.

Kaela stiffened. She knew that voice.

Captain Aldric stepped into the dim light, his arms folded across his broad chest. He looked down at her with an expression she couldn't quite read—calm, measured, like a man who had expected this outcome all along.

Kaela fought the urge to spit at his feet.

"You betrayed me," she said, her voice hoarse.

Aldric tilted his head. "Did I?"

She yanked at the shackles, the cold iron biting into her skin. "You let me walk into a trap."

Aldric sighed, kneeling before her so they were at eye level. "I never lied to you, Kaela. I told you my loyalty was to the crown."

Kaela's breath came short and fast. "That crown belongs to Raelan."

Aldric's expression didn't change. "Does it?"

Something about his tone sent a cold shiver down her spine.

She swallowed hard. "What do you want?"

Aldric studied her for a long moment before standing. "You, my dear thief, are a valuable piece in this game. And my king has decided you should live—for now."

She clenched her fists. "If you think I'm going to beg for my life—"

Aldric chuckled. "Oh, I know you won't. But perhaps you'll reconsider once you see the world outside this cell."

Kaela narrowed her eyes.

Aldric rapped his knuckles against the iron bars, and within moments, the heavy door behind him groaned open. Two guards stepped inside, their hands resting on the hilts of their swords.

"Bring her," Aldric ordered.

Rough hands yanked Kaela to her feet, dragging her forward. She forced herself to keep her breathing steady, her mind working through possible escapes. But without her weapons, her strength, or any sense of where she was in the castle, she was out of options.

For now.

The guards led her through a series of dimly lit corridors, past narrow slits of windows where golden light spilled in. The air grew warmer, richer with the scent of burning candles and expensive oils. She was being taken out of the dungeons.

That meant they wanted her to see something.

Her suspicions were confirmed when the guards led her into a grand hall.

Massive chandeliers cast flickering light across polished marble floors, and thick red banners bearing the sigil of the golden wolf hung from towering columns. Courtiers lined the sides of the hall, their whispers hushed as she was dragged forward.

At the far end, seated upon the gilded throne, was King Alric the Usurper.

And standing beside him—his expression unreadable—was Raelan.

Kaela froze.

Her pulse pounded in her ears, but she forced herself to keep her face impassive.

Raelan's gaze met hers for only a moment before shifting away. His posture was stiff, his hands curled into tight fists at his sides.

The guards forced her to kneel before the throne.

King Alric leaned forward, his sharp eyes gleaming with amusement. He was older than the last painting she had seen of him, but the cruelty in his face was unmistakable.

"A thief," he mused, tapping his fingers against the armrest. "And yet, you were found sneaking through my castle like a little mouse in the walls. Tell me, girl, did you truly think you could steal from me?"

Kaela gritted her teeth, refusing to speak.

The king smiled. "Ah. Silent, are we? No matter. I have no need for your words—I know exactly what you were after."

He gestured to one of his advisors, who stepped forward and unfurled a parchment. Kaela's stomach twisted as she recognized the document—it was the ledger she had been trying to steal.

The king's eyes flickered toward Raelan.

"This was meant for you, wasn't it?"

Raelan didn't answer.

The king chuckled. "Oh, my dear nephew. You always were too sentimental."

Kaela inhaled sharply. Nephew.

Her mind spun as she tried to make sense of the scene before her. Raelan wasn't in chains. He wasn't being held prisoner. He was standing freely in the royal court.

And the way the courtiers looked at him—it wasn't with

suspicion. It was with expectation.

Her stomach turned cold.

"You knew," she whispered, her voice barely audible.

Raelan flinched.

The king laughed, the sound rich with amusement. "Ah, so the little thief finally realizes the truth."

Kaela's nails dug into her palms. "You made a deal."

Raelan's eyes snapped to hers, his expression unreadable.

The king's voice was smooth as silk. "You thought my dear nephew would be so foolish as to wage war against me with no hope of victory? No, no, my dear girl. Raelan understands the cost of power."

Kaela couldn't breathe.

Raelan had surrendered.

She had risked everything—had stepped into a den of wolves— because she had believed in him. And now he stood before her, not as a fugitive, but as a man welcomed back into the fold.

The king's grin widened. "My nephew has chosen the path of wisdom. He has agreed to return to his rightful place within my court. And, as a reward, I have granted him a betrothal."

The court murmured in approval.

Kaela forced herself to look at Raelan. "Betrothal?"

His jaw was tight, his gaze dark. "To Lady Evelyne of House Valtoris."

Kaela felt like the world had tilted beneath her feet.

Evelyne. A name she knew well. The daughter of the most powerful noble house in Whitecliff. The woman who had once been promised to Raelan, long before the coup that had stolen his throne.

Bile rose in Kaela's throat.

The king leaned forward. "You see, thief, there was never a need for rebellion. The throne does not have to be taken by force—it can be secured with alliances."

Kaela barely heard him. She could only stare at Raelan, searching for something—anything—that told her he wasn't truly a part of this.

But Raelan said nothing.

The weight of betrayal settled deep in her bones.

The king smirked. "Take her back to the dungeons. We'll decide what to do with her later."

The guards seized her arms.

Kaela barely felt them.

She had been played.

Raelan had made his choice.

And she was nothing more than a loose end in a game far greater than she had ever realized.

Seven

A Dangerous Masquerade

The air inside the ballroom was thick with perfume, the scent mingling with the sounds of muted laughter and soft music. Candles flickered along the edges of the grand hall, casting long, shifting shadows against the polished floors. The walls were draped with rich tapestries, their golden threads shimmering faintly in the low light. The hall was filled with the glitter of wealth—silk gowns, velvet cloaks, diamonds in every ear, every neck, every wrist. But underneath the glittering surface, there was something darker, something more dangerous that Kaela could feel pressing against her chest with every step she took.

The masquerade had begun.

Kaela stood just inside the ballroom's entrance, her hand pressed against the doorframe, her pulse hammering in her ears.

She was cloaked in a disguise so elaborate that even her own reflection would scarcely recognize her. The mask she wore was made of silver and lace, adorned with intricate patterns and delicate pearls. Her gown was the color of midnight, woven with threads that caught the light in a way that made it seem like she was shrouded in shadows. She looked every bit the noblewoman—untouchable, flawless, playing her part in the game of masks and lies.

And yet, beneath the layers of silk and lace, she could feel the weight of the key still tucked in her pocket—the key that had cost her everything.

Her eyes scanned the room, taking in the scene with careful precision. The courtiers were mingling, their voices lilting and light as they complimented one another on their costumes and fine wine. But Kaela knew better than to be fooled by the polished smiles and the soft words. Behind every smile was a dagger, behind every flattering comment was a secret.

It was a game of masks.

But there was one person who she had not seen yet.

Raelan.

She swallowed, her throat dry. It had been days since the betrothal had been announced—days since she had seen him standing beside his uncle, a crown in one hand, a broken heart in the other. Days since she had walked into the trap that had been set for her, a pawn in a game she had no understanding of.

The doors to the ballroom opened with a soft creak, and a hush swept through the crowd.

Raelan entered.

He stood tall, his broad shoulders framed by the regal cut of his coat, the dark fabric embroidered with silver threads that caught the light. His mask, a simple black design, was adorned with golden accents, highlighting the sharp angles of his face. His hair, slightly longer than it had been before, fell around his face in a way that only made his presence more commanding. The murmurs that followed him were almost imperceptible, but Kaela could hear them all the same—hushed whispers of admiration, of curiosity, of speculation.

Raelan made his way toward the center of the room, where his uncle stood, waiting. King Alric wore an elaborate mask of his own, a golden lion's face that gleamed under the chandeliers. The two of them stood together, a vision of power and promise, the future of Whitecliff resting on the fragile thread of their alliance.

Kaela's stomach turned.

But there was no time for hesitation. She had come here for a reason. She had come here to find the truth, to uncover the lies that had ensnared them all.

She moved through the crowd, her steps purposeful, her eyes

locked on Raelan as he spoke with his uncle, their voices low, their words lost to the hum of the crowd around them. She could see the tension between them, the barely concealed animosity that flickered in Raelan's eyes whenever he glanced at his uncle. The weight of duty pressed down on him, but it was not the duty of a king—it was the duty of a man who had been betrayed.

Kaela reached the table where drinks were being served, her fingers brushing against the crystal goblets as she passed. The wine was rich, dark, like blood, but it didn't interest her. What she needed was information, something she could use. She needed a way to get closer to the prince, to find out what was really happening behind the glittering mask of the kingdom.

Her gaze flickered to the side, and that's when she saw him— Captain Aldric.

The sight of him was enough to make her heart skip a beat. She had known from the moment she had stepped into the ballroom that things were never as simple as they seemed. Aldric was no fool, and neither was she. If he had come to this masquerade, then he was here for a reason.

Her eyes locked with his for just a moment, and she could see the subtle shift in his posture. He didn't move, but his eyes— dark and calculating—followed her every step. He knew exactly what she was doing.

And for a moment, she wondered if he was there to stop her.

But she couldn't afford to stop now.

Taking a deep breath, Kaela adjusted her mask, slipping deeper into the crowd. She moved like a shadow, unnoticed and unseen, until she was standing near the grand staircase where Raelan and his uncle stood talking. Their conversation was still too low for her to hear, but she could see the tension between them. There was something off about this whole evening. Something didn't add up.

Her hand slipped into her pocket, and she grasped the key. It was cold, like a dead thing.

The faintest glint of gold caught her eye.

Raelan.

He was looking at her now.

For a moment, everything around her faded. The noise, the laughter, the whispers—they all seemed distant. All she could hear was the rhythmic beating of her heart and the weight of his gaze.

And then, without a word, he began to move toward her.

Her breath caught in her throat as she watched him approach, his strides long and purposeful. His eyes never left hers, and it was as if the entire ballroom had disappeared, leaving only the two of them standing in the middle of it.

When he reached her, he stopped. There was a long, charged silence between them. She couldn't read the expression on his face, but there was something in his eyes—something that made her heart flutter.

"You shouldn't be here," he whispered, his voice low, just for her.

Kaela's lips parted, but no words came out. She couldn't respond. What could she say?

"You need to leave," he continued, his gaze flicking over her shoulder, as if to make sure no one was watching them. "You don't know what you're getting yourself into."

"Do I?" Kaela replied, her voice a touch sharper than she intended. She raised her chin slightly, defiant, even as her heart raced. "I think I know exactly what I'm getting into. But what about you, Raelan? Do you really know what you've become?"

He flinched, the words striking deeper than she thought.

Before he could respond, the king's voice boomed from across the room. "Raelan! Come here."

Raelan's jaw clenched. He turned away from her, his back rigid. But before he walked away, he met her eyes once more.

"If you don't leave now," he said quietly, his voice carrying only to her, "I can't help you."

Kaela felt her stomach drop.

She stood there, frozen for a moment, as the crowd swirled around her, their laughter and music suddenly distant, their voices just background noise.

She had come to this masquerade expecting answers. But what she had found was a man trapped in a web of lies and betrayal, tangled in a web he couldn't escape.

And she realized then—perhaps too late—that she, too, was caught in the same web.

Eight

Blades and Broken Promises

T he moon hung heavy in the sky, its pale light casting long shadows over the castle courtyard. The wind was cold tonight, biting through the layers of silk and velvet that draped the nobles in opulence. But Kaela felt none of the chill. Instead, her body burned with the heat of betrayal, the ache of broken promises, and the sharp edge of her purpose.

The masquerade had ended, the guests now scattered throughout the castle. The night had grown darker, more intimate, as whispers and secrets exchanged hands beneath the flickering candlelight. Kaela had felt the weight of those secrets pressing against her chest all evening, suffocating her with every step she took. But nothing had prepared her for the encounter that followed—the one where she had finally seen Raelan, really seen him, standing by his uncle's side as if the man were his blood, as if the throne belonged to anyone but the rightful heir.

His words echoed in her mind, too soft and too cold. You don't know what you're getting yourself into.

Kaela knew he was right. She didn't know. Not yet.

But she would.

She was tired of being played. Tired of being the pawn in someone else's game.

She made her way through the darkened halls, the sound of her footsteps muffled by the thick carpets underfoot. The guards were few tonight—another sign of the evening's unspoken significance. No doubt the court would be focused on the festivities, and that left her the perfect opportunity to act. She was already so deep in the castle that retreat was no longer an option. Her only choice was to move forward.

She reached the narrow hallway that led to the royal quarters, a place rarely seen by anyone not of noble blood. She moved quickly, her heart pounding in her chest, her mind racing with thoughts of the ledger, the key, the records that could expose the full scope of her uncle's treachery.

At the far end of the hall stood the door she was searching for. The chamber beyond was rumored to hold the most damning evidence of all—the records that chronicled every decision made in the royal court, every alliance, every betrayal. But more importantly, it would hold the truth about Raelan's father, the late king, and what had really happened during the coup. If Kaela could uncover the secrets locked away in that room, she would have the leverage she needed.

She paused before the door, her breath steady despite the storm raging inside her. She didn't need to pick the lock this time—the key Aldric had given her had worked wonders. With one swift motion, she turned the handle and pushed the door open.

The room inside was small and dimly lit by a single candle that flickered on a desk cluttered with maps and papers. The air smelled faintly of ink and parchment, and the only sound in the space was the quiet rustle of papers as they fluttered under the weight of the breeze.

She stepped inside, closing the door behind her with care. The room was as quiet as the grave. Her eyes quickly adjusted to the low light, scanning the room for the records she needed. She moved toward a wooden cabinet against the far wall, its shelves stacked high with leather-bound tomes and scrolls, each one more precious than the last.

But just as she reached out to open the cabinet, the door to the chamber swung open, and a cold, commanding voice sliced through the silence.

"Looking for something?"

Kaela's heart stopped.

She turned slowly, the blood in her veins turning to ice. Raelan stood in the doorway, framed by the dim light from the hall, his posture stiff, his eyes narrowed. He was dressed in the same dark attire he had worn at the masquerade, though now his mask was gone. His gaze swept over her, taking in every detail—every movement. And for the first time, Kaela saw the weight of his choices in his eyes.

"You shouldn't be here," he said, his voice flat, emotionless.

Kaela's pulse quickened, but she didn't flinch. "I could say the same to you."

Raelan didn't move. "What is it you're looking for, Kaela? What are you trying to uncover?"

Her fingers clenched around the edge of the cabinet. "The truth."

"Truth?" He scoffed, stepping further into the room. "You think you can find it in those records? That they'll tell you what happened? What really happened?" His eyes darkened, and for a brief moment, Kaela saw something else in him—something that didn't belong to the prince she had once known. "You won't find what you're looking for. You'll only find what they want you to."

Kaela's heart slammed against her ribcage. She took a step back. "You knew?"

Raelan's gaze flickered, his jaw tightening. He didn't answer her immediately, but when he spoke, his voice was cold, distant. "I knew what the cost of my return would be. I knew that to take back what was rightfully mine, I would have to—"

"You would have to betray everything you ever stood for?" Kaela cut him off, her voice rising in disbelief. "Your father? Your people? Your own blood?" She took a step forward, her eyes locked on his. "Raelan, this isn't you. This isn't the man I once knew."

His expression shifted, a flicker of pain passing through his features before it was quickly masked. He took a step toward her, his presence overwhelming. "You don't understand. You never understood the choice I had to make."

Kaela's fists clenched. "I understand perfectly. You chose him. You chose the throne over everything you said you cared about. Over me."

Raelan's eyes darkened. "It wasn't a choice between you and the throne, Kaela. It was a choice between my kingdom and my life. And I chose my kingdom."

"Your kingdom?" Kaela's voice cracked. "You've traded everything—everyone—for a crown. And for what? To become your uncle's puppet?"

Raelan stepped closer, his breath warm against her skin. "You don't know the weight of this, Kaela. You don't know what it means to carry the burden of a kingdom on your shoulders. You think this is some game? You think you can just walk away from everything you've ever known?"

Kaela's eyes burned with unshed tears. "Maybe that's because I don't have a kingdom to carry. Maybe I don't have the luxury of choosing who I am based on a throne or a crown. I never did."

For a moment, they stood in silence, the tension between them thick and suffocating.

And then, without warning, Raelan's hand shot out, gripping her wrist with such force that she gasped. His face was inches from hers, and for a brief second, Kaela saw the conflict within him—his internal war, the battle he had fought in silence, the sacrifice he had made.

"I had no choice," he muttered, his voice low, haunted. "I had to make a choice, Kaela. Between my blood and my honor, between what was right and what was necessary."

Kaela's heart pounded in her chest, but her anger flared. "And what about us, Raelan? What about the promise we made to each other? Does that mean nothing to you?"

His grip tightened, and for a moment, it seemed like he might speak, might give her the answer she needed. But instead, his gaze darkened, his eyes hardening. "The promise I made to you was a lie. The world doesn't work the way we want it to, Kaela. The world doesn't care about promises. It cares about power. It always has."

Before she could respond, he thrust her back against the cabinet with a sudden force, pushing her off balance. The cold edge of the wooden surface dug into her back, and her breath caught in her throat.

Raelan's face was inches from hers. The air between them crackled with unsaid words, broken dreams, and the tension of a love that had once seemed unbreakable but now lay shattered at their feet.

Kaela's hand found the hilt of a dagger—her dagger. She had hidden it, tucked away in her sleeve when the guards had bound her.

Before Raelan could react, Kaela drew the blade and pressed it to his throat, her pulse roaring in her ears.

"Don't come any closer," she said, her voice a whisper of steel.

Raelan didn't flinch. "You'll kill me, then?" he asked, his voice steady despite the blade at his throat. "After everything, after us?"

Kaela's heart twisted. She hesitated, the blade trembling in her grip, but her resolve hardened. "I would never kill you, Raelan," she said, her voice barely above a whisper. "But I will never forgive you either."

For a long moment, neither of them moved.

Then, with a single, fluid motion, Raelan stepped back, his hands raised in surrender. "Then you should leave," he said quietly. "Before the rest of the world does what I cannot."

Kaela's breath caught in her throat as she realized the truth.

The man she had once loved—the prince who had promised her a future—was gone.

59

Nine

The Thief's Past Unveiled

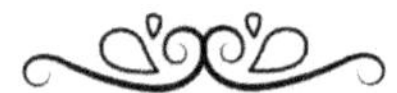

Kaela had always believed that the shadows were her home—that she was untouchable in the dark, a creature of the night who lived between the cracks of the world. She had spent years hiding, slipping through the underbelly of Whitecliff and beyond, surviving on nothing but her wits and her skill with a blade. But now, standing in the cold, stone-walled chamber beneath the castle, with the echoes of Raelan's words still ringing in her ears, she realized how little she truly knew about herself.

The door slammed shut behind her, the heavy thud reverberating through the narrow corridor. She didn't flinch, didn't look back. She had no time to waste. The dungeon was no longer her destination—it was the past, the memories she had tried so desperately to forget.

The stone walls around her were damp, their surface covered in a thin layer of moss, like the remnants of a dream she no longer cared to hold onto. A single torch flickered in the corner, casting eerie shadows across the chamber. The air was stale, the faint scent of decay mingling with the distant sound of dripping water. She moved deeper into the chamber, her boots silent on the stone floor.

She had made a decision, a dangerous one, to leave the man who had once promised her everything. Raelan's betrayal wasn't just a blow to her heart—it was a dagger to everything she had ever believed about herself. She had lived in the shadows for so long, hiding from the world and from the consequences of her actions. But there was no running anymore.

No more lies.

No more games.

She pulled back her cloak, revealing the worn leather vest she had been wearing for years. Her fingers brushed over the familiar markings etched into the fabric—a series of old scars, not just from the many close calls of her life, but from something deeper, something more painful.

Before she could think any longer, a low, gravelly voice echoed from the darkness.

"You've come."

Kaela stiffened, the hairs on the back of her neck standing on end. Her hand instinctively went to the hilt of her dagger, but the voice stopped her before she could pull it free.

"You didn't think I'd forget you, did you?" the voice asked, a cold, mocking tone threading through the words.

Kaela's heart skipped. She knew that voice.

"I didn't think I'd ever hear from you again," she replied, her voice strained, barely above a whisper.

From the darkness, a figure stepped forward, his tall, imposing frame becoming clearer under the dim torchlight. He was dressed in black, the shadows seeming to cling to him like a cloak. His face was sharp, his jaw set in a permanent scowl, but it was his eyes—cold and unfeeling—that made Kaela's breath catch in her throat.

"Roderick." Her voice was a mere rasp. She didn't know whether to run or stand her ground.

He smiled, but it was a smile devoid of warmth. A smile that was more like a grimace than anything resembling happiness.

"Did you think I wouldn't find you?" he asked, stepping closer. "That I would forget the one who betrayed me?"

She clenched her fists, forcing herself to stay calm. Her heart pounded in her chest, but she didn't show fear. She couldn't afford to.

"I didn't betray you, Roderick," she said, her voice stronger this time, though the tremor in her hand betrayed her. "You made your choice. You knew what it would cost you."

He took another step forward, his boots heavy on the stone floor. "And you didn't think it would cost you, too?" His eyes narrowed. "You think you can walk away from the life you built? From everything you've done?"

Kaela didn't respond. She didn't need to. She knew exactly what he meant.

It had been years since she had last seen Roderick—the man who had once been everything to her. The man who had taken her in when she was a lost, frightened girl, and shown her the ways of the world. The man who had taught her to steal, to survive, to fight for herself when no one else would. But he had also taught her something far darker. Roderick had given her power, but at a price.

The memories came flooding back, more vivid and sharp than she ever expected.

—-

It had all started when she was only a child, barely fifteen, hungry and cold on the streets of Whitecliff. She had been an orphan, living in the gutters, stealing scraps to survive. She had no family, no home, no purpose—until she met Roderick.

He had been a thief, a shadow in the night who moved like a

phantom, always unseen, always elusive. He had approached her one winter's night, offering her warmth and food in exchange for her loyalty. She hadn't trusted him at first—how could she?—but hunger had a way of silencing even the loudest of doubts.

Roderick had been the first person to show her the ropes. How to pick pockets, how to slip into rich houses unnoticed, how to talk her way into places where others would be thrown out without a second thought. She had learned quickly. She had become his protégé, and over time, she had grown more skilled, more confident.

They were unstoppable, she had thought. Together, they ruled the shadows of Whitecliff, taking what they wanted without hesitation, without remorse. She had never questioned Roderick's methods. He was the leader, the mastermind, and she was his apprentice.

But then the greed had started to grow. Not in her, but in him. And that was where the trouble had begun.

—-

Kaela's hands tightened around the edge of the cabinet as Roderick's words pulled her from the memory.

"You were never meant to be just another thief, Kaela," he said, his voice low and dangerous. "I gave you everything. I showed you how to take what you wanted. I made you who you are."

Kaela shook her head, her chest tightening. "You made me a monster, Roderick," she spat. "You showed me how to survive, but you also showed me how to destroy everything I cared about. How to ruin everything I've ever loved."

Roderick's eyes glinted in the darkness. "And you think you've changed? You think you've walked away from the person you were? That he"—he gestured toward the castle above them—"has changed you?"

Kaela's breath caught in her throat. "What does Raelan have to do with this?"

Roderick smiled, a dark, bitter smile. "You've always been good at running away from your past, Kaela. But it doesn't let you go that easily. It never does." He stepped closer, his hand outstretched, his fingers brushing against her cheek. "You've spent your whole life pretending you were someone else. But we both know the truth."

Kaela felt a chill crawl up her spine. "Stop," she whispered, but her voice lacked the strength she needed.

"No," Roderick's voice dropped to a hiss, his hand coming to rest on her shoulder, his grip tightening. "You never stopped being mine, Kaela. And you never will."

—-

Kaela's breath faltered, her mind reeling. The weight of Roderick's words crushed her, dragging her back into the past she had fought so hard to bury. She had thought she could leave it behind, thought she could outrun him, but she hadn't. Not really.

She had tried to forget what he had done to her. To them.

But in that moment, Kaela knew the truth. She had never been free.

And now, Roderick had come to remind her of it.

—-

"You can't hide from me, Kaela," he said, his grip on her shoulder growing tighter. "Not now. Not ever."

She flinched but held her ground. "I'm not hiding from you," she said, forcing her voice steady. "But I won't let you control me anymore. Not now, not ever."

Roderick's face darkened, his grip loosening as he stepped back. "You think you've won? You think you've made a new life for yourself?" His laugh was harsh and bitter. "You're nothing, Kaela. You always were. Just a thief."

"I'm more than that," she said quietly, her voice cold and determined. "I've learned what it means to fight for myself. To choose who I am." She stepped toward him, eyes flashing with the fire of someone who had nothing left to lose. "And I choose to leave you in the past where you belong."

Roderick's eyes flickered with something between rage and disbelief. "You'll never be free of me," he spat. "No matter what you think, I'll always own you."

Kaela took another step forward, the words that followed coming from deep within her. "Not anymore."

And with that, she turned on her heel, walking away from the man who had once been her world, her mentor, her curse. She walked away from the shadows of her past and into the unknown.

Ten

A Battle of Loyalties

The wind howled through the narrow corridors of the castle, sending the faint scent of blood and betrayal curling into the air. Kaela stood alone at the edge of the courtyard, her hand gripping the hilt of her dagger so tightly that her knuckles had turned white. The night had settled into a thick, suffocating silence, the kind that only preceded the storm.

Her breath came in shallow gasps as she watched the castle walls in the distance, her mind racing with thoughts of Raelan, of Roderick, and the choices she had yet to make. In one corner of the world, her past called her back with the weight of every crime she'd ever committed, every lie she'd ever told. In the other, Raelan stood as the prince of a kingdom, a man bound by duty, by blood. They were both things she had once believed in—both things that now threatened to pull her apart at the seams.

"Kaela."

The voice startled her, its low, familiar tone slicing through the tension like a blade. She didn't need to turn around to know who it was. She had been waiting for this moment, dreading it even more than she had feared Roderick's return.

Raelan stepped into her line of sight, his figure a silhouette against the faint glow of the castle. His mask was gone, but the cold, calculating edge to his eyes had not softened. He had always worn the weight of his birth like a shackle, but tonight, it was heavier than ever. She saw it in the way his shoulders were squared, the way his jaw was set tight. There was something in him now, something that felt even more distant than the prince she had once known.

Kaela forced herself to meet his gaze, her heart pounding in her chest.

"You should go," she said, her voice low but firm. "Before it's too late."

Raelan raised an eyebrow, his expression unreadable. "Too late for what?"

Kaela took a step back, her eyes flickering toward the shadows where Roderick's presence lingered, just out of sight but impossible to ignore. "You don't understand," she began, her voice barely above a whisper. "I didn't come here to be part of this. I didn't come here to play your games, to be your pawn."

Raelan took a slow step forward, his eyes narrowing. "You think I want to use you, Kaela? You think I want you to be part of this—part of my world?"

Kaela bit her lip, the words getting stuck in her throat. She didn't know what he wanted anymore. She didn't know what he had become.

"I thought I knew you, Raelan," she said, her voice breaking on the last word. "I thought I understood who you were. But now… now you've become something else."

He stopped in front of her, too close—too close to the person she had once loved. His presence pressed in on her like the weight of the whole castle, suffocating. His voice was softer now, but there was a hardness in it that sent a chill through her veins.

"You don't understand," he repeated, his tone sharper this time. "The choices I've had to make… the things I've had to do… They weren't easy, Kaela. But they were necessary. You think I wanted to betray you? You think I wanted to sacrifice us? You think I wanted to stand by his side?"

She shook her head, her throat tight. "Then why did you? Why didn't you fight for us, for your people, for everything you said you believed in?"

Raelan looked away, his jaw tightening. "I had no choice."

The words hung in the air between them like a veil, pulling them further apart. Kaela wanted to scream. She wanted to shake him, to make him see reason. But she could see it in his eyes—the cold certainty that his decisions had been made long before she had ever entered his life.

"Raelan…" She whispered his name as though it could break through the wall he had built between them, but there was no softness in his gaze. He had already made his decision.

"You've chosen him," she said, her voice heavy with the weight of that simple truth. "You've chosen the crown. And you've chosen him."

Raelan's eyes flickered toward the shadows, toward the distant figure of Roderick lurking just beyond the edge of the courtyard. "You don't know what you're asking," he said, his voice strained, his fists clenched. "I've sacrificed everything—everything—for this kingdom. I didn't have the luxury of making choices that were easy."

"I don't care about your kingdom," Kaela snapped, her voice shaking. "You sold your soul for it. And now you're going to watch it burn."

Raelan took a step back, his face hardening. "Then walk away. Leave. Go back to the life you knew. Go back to the shadows. I won't stop you."

Kaela's heart clenched in her chest, the words searing through her. She had come so far. She had given everything, risked everything, only to be confronted by the same emptiness she had tried so hard to escape. She looked at Raelan, the man she had once trusted, once loved, and saw nothing but the cold, calculating prince who had chosen power over everything.

"I can't walk away from this, Raelan," she whispered. "You've already taken everything I ever had."

The silence that followed was deafening. Raelan's gaze softened for just a moment, but it was gone before Kaela could react. He turned, his back to her, his shoulders tense. His voice was a mere whisper on the wind.

"If you stay, Kaela… there's no going back."

She shook her head, her eyes burning with unshed tears. "I never wanted to go back. I wanted to fight. I wanted to believe that there was still a chance for us… for you."

Raelan didn't answer. He simply turned and walked away, his footsteps echoing in the cold night. Kaela stood frozen, her breath catching in her throat. Every part of her screamed to follow him, to beg him to turn back, to remind him of the man he had once been. But she couldn't. She wouldn't.

The sound of footsteps behind her made her turn.

Roderick.

He stepped out of the shadows, his face unreadable beneath the dark, blood-red mask that hid everything he was. She felt a shiver run down her spine as he approached, his figure looming like a predator closing in on its prey.

"You've made your choice, haven't you?" Roderick's voice was quiet, almost gentle, but the malice in it was unmistakable.

Kaela's grip tightened on the dagger at her waist. She had never been more afraid of him, but she would be damned if she let him see it.

"You've always been good at making choices, haven't you?" Kaela said, her voice colder than the wind that swept through the courtyard. "Choosing power over people. Choosing control over loyalty."

Roderick smiled, that same cruel smile he had always worn when he thought he had the upper hand. "I never had a choice, Kaela. I've always done what needed to be done." He stepped closer, his voice lowering. "And you? You've always been a tool to be used. First by me, and now by him."

Kaela's breath quickened. "What do you want from me?"

Roderick's eyes glinted with something dark, something dangerous. "I want you to understand that you've never been in control. You've never been free."

"I'm not like you, Roderick," she spat. "I never was."

He tilted his head, studying her. "Then you're a fool." His voice grew darker. "Because in the end, Kaela, we all make the same choice. We either bend the knee to power, or we die trying to take it for ourselves."

A tense silence filled the space between them, the air thick with the weight of unspoken truths. Kaela felt the weight of Roderick's words, but she wouldn't let him break her. She had walked away from him once. She would do it again.

"I'll never be your pawn again," she said, her voice cold as ice. "You don't control me. You never did."

Roderick's smile faltered, and for a brief moment, Kaela saw the man beneath the mask—the man she had once known. But it was fleeting, lost in the darkness.

"Then you're already lost," he whispered, his eyes glinting with malice.

Before she could react, he turned, his cloak swirling around him as he vanished into the shadows.

Kaela stood in the silence, her heart heavy with the weight of the choices she had made, the choices yet to come. Raelan had chosen his kingdom. Roderick had chosen power.

And her?

Her choice had yet to be made.

Eleven

A Kiss That Shouldn't Have Happened

T he rain came like a torrent, drenching everything it touched, soaking the stone of the castle walls and the earth beneath Kaela's feet. She stood at the edge of the battlements, her cloak drawn tight around her shoulders, trying to shield herself from the storm. The cold wind whipped through her hair, but it didn't bother her—not now. The chill in the air was nothing compared to the chill that had settled in her heart since the events of the past days had unfolded.

Raelan. Roderick. The kingdom.

She had come so close to making sense of everything, only to find herself deeper in the tangled web of lies and broken promises than ever before. Her mind raced as she replayed the moment with Raelan—the moment where everything had changed. She had thought she understood him, had believed that their bond was something that could never be broken. But now, she was left standing alone on the precipice, wondering if she had ever truly known him at all.

The sound of footsteps behind her made her stiffen. She didn't have to turn around to know who it was. She could feel the presence of the man, the weight of him, pressing against her as he closed the distance between them.

"Kaela."

Raelan's voice was low, filled with something she couldn't quite place. It was softer than it had been in their last encounter, less guarded. Still, it made her blood run cold. She didn't know if it was because of what had happened between them—or what was about to.

She turned, keeping her face impassive, her eyes cold. But inside, her heart was a wild thing, thrumming like a trapped bird against her ribcage.

"You shouldn't be here," she said, her voice barely above a whisper. It wasn't a plea, not exactly. It was more a warning—something both of them understood.

Raelan stopped a few feet away, standing in the rain, his eyes dark and unreadable. His hair was wet, clinging to his face, but he didn't seem to care. His gaze never wavered from hers.

"I needed to talk to you," he said, his words slow, deliberate.

Kaela's pulse quickened, but she forced herself to remain still. "There's nothing to talk about."

He took a step closer, his boots soft against the stone floor. His presence filled the space between them, suffocating, demanding. "I know you're angry, Kaela. I know I've hurt you. But I need you to understand."

"Understand what?" she cut him off, her voice rising despite herself. "Understand that you've betrayed everything we ever were? Understand that you've chosen him over me—over everything? Understand that you've given up the very thing that made you human for a throne you didn't even want?"

Raelan's eyes flashed with something dangerous, something familiar. His jaw tightened, and for a moment, Kaela thought he might snap, might lash out in anger. But instead, he stood there, silent, the weight of his choices hanging heavy between them.

"I did what I had to do," he said quietly, his voice raw. "I didn't have a choice, Kaela. You know that."

She shook her head, tears welling up in her eyes, but she refused to let them fall. She would not let him see her weak, would not give him that satisfaction. "You always had a choice, Raelan. You just didn't want to make it."

He reached out then, his fingers brushing against her arm in a fleeting touch, but it was enough to send a shiver through her. She stiffened, but he didn't pull back. Instead, he stepped closer, until their bodies were nearly touching.

For a long moment, they stood there, neither of them speaking, the rain pouring down around them, drenching them both. Kaela could feel the heat of his body against hers, could feel the tension in the air between them. It was suffocating. Electric.

And then, before she could stop herself, she reached out and touched his face.

Raelan's eyes widened in surprise, but he didn't pull away. His hand came up to cover hers, his touch warm, grounding. It was a simple gesture, but it was enough to crack the dam that had held her back from everything she had been feeling.

In that moment, everything else faded. The kingdom, the betrayal, the lies—they all dissolved into the background, leaving only the two of them standing there, soaked to the bone, their breaths ragged in the cold air.

Kaela's heart pounded, each beat louder than the last as she stared into his eyes, searching for something—anything—that would tell her that the man she had once loved was still inside. That he wasn't gone, wasn't lost to the power and the crown.

Raelan's thumb brushed over her wrist, the faintest touch, but it was enough to send a jolt of electricity through her.

"Kaela," he whispered, his voice thick, hoarse, as though he, too, was struggling to keep control. "I never wanted this. I never wanted to hurt you."

Kaela swallowed hard, her breath catching in her throat. "Then why did you do it?"

Raelan stepped even closer, his body now mere inches from hers. He reached up, his hand cupping her face with surprising tenderness, and Kaela's breath hitched in her chest.

"I didn't want to hurt you, Kaela. But there are things I cannot change. Things I cannot undo," he said, his voice so soft, so raw that it broke her heart all over again.

Her lips parted, but the words got stuck, tangled in the wreckage of what had been and what was no longer. She had wanted him to say it—to say that he loved her, that it hadn't all been a lie. But he didn't. He couldn't.

And still, in that moment, she found herself leaning into him, into the warmth of his touch, the familiarity of him, despite everything that had happened between them.

Her lips brushed against his before she could think, before she could stop herself. It was a kiss that shouldn't have happened— a kiss born of desperation, of need, of a shared history that neither of them could escape.

Raelan didn't pull away.

Instead, his hand slid to the back of her neck, pulling her closer, deepening the kiss, and Kaela's heart shattered. She had told herself she was done with him, done with the lies and the broken promises, but the feel of him against her, the taste of him on her lips, made everything she had fought for seem like it didn't matter anymore.

For a moment, it was just them—the two of them in the rain, as if the world around them didn't exist, as if nothing else mattered. She kissed him like she was starving, like the kiss was the only thing that could save her from the mess they had created.

But when they pulled apart, it wasn't relief she felt. It wasn't the bliss she had imagined. It was the same suffocating weight that had been there before—the weight of betrayal, of choices made, of a love that couldn't survive the world they lived in.

Raelan's forehead rested against hers, his breath coming in shallow gasps. "I'm sorry, Kaela," he whispered, his voice breaking.

Kaela shook her head, pulling away from him. Her hands trembled at her sides, the shock of the kiss still reverberating through her, but now it felt like a betrayal of its own.

"You don't get to apologize to me," she whispered, her voice tight with restraint. "Not after everything."

Raelan stepped back, his eyes pleading, but Kaela didn't want to look at him anymore. She couldn't.

"I can't do this," she said, her voice hoarse. "I can't keep pretending that we can just go back to what we were. We can't fix this. Not anymore."

He stood there, his expression raw, vulnerable in a way she had never seen before. But it didn't matter. The distance between them wasn't just physical anymore. It was everything.

Without another word, Kaela turned and walked away, her heart pounding in her chest. The rain poured down, but it didn't matter. Nothing mattered.

She had kissed him, and it had broken her. And now, there was no going back.

Twelve

A Coronation in Blood

The castle was alive with whispers. The sound of silk rustling against marble floors, the clinking of fine silverware, and the distant hum of music filled the air. But beneath all of it—the opulent decorations, the regal faces adorned with masks of gold—there was a palpable sense of tension. A storm was coming.

Kaela stood at the edge of the grand hall, hidden among the shadows of the towering columns. She had been here countless times before, slipping between the cracks of the royal court, watching as the nobles of Whitecliff strutted around, their faces painted with smiles as false as their allegiances. But tonight was different. The air was thick with anticipation. Tonight, everything would change.

Tonight, Raelan would be crowned.

The coronation was an event unlike any other, a spectacle of power and wealth that drew the finest lords and ladies from every corner of the kingdom. White and gold banners hung from the high walls, the castle's greatest treasures displayed like trophies. The long hall was filled with people—councilors, diplomats, nobles from the great houses—all there to witness the crowning of a prince who had spent ten long years in exile. His return had been nothing short of miraculous, but tonight, it would be more than that. Tonight, Raelan would reclaim his birthright.

But the whispers… they weren't just about Raelan. They weren't just about his triumphant return. They were about the blood. The blood that would stain the coronation.

Kaela felt the weight of those whispers pressing against her. Her heart raced with every footstep she heard approaching, every rustle of silk as the courtiers passed by. They all had their roles to play tonight, but Kaela? She wasn't here to watch. She wasn't here to celebrate. She was here to stop a disaster.

She hadn't come all this way, hadn't risked everything, just to watch Raelan put on the crown and become what his uncle had always intended for him: another puppet in the game of kings. She had seen the way he'd looked at her, the way he'd acted like everything—everything—was already decided. But it wasn't. Not yet.

The door at the far end of the hall opened, and a hush fell over the crowd.

Raelan entered.

He was magnificent. His dark, intricate robes shimmered under the golden light, the deep reds and blacks of his attire drawing the eye to his tall frame. The crown was yet to be placed upon his head, but he wore it already—an invisible crown made of duty and obligation. His eyes, dark and haunted, scanned the room. For a moment, their gazes met—Kaela's heart lurched, but she forced herself not to look away. She wasn't here for him. She wasn't here for that lost promise between them.

Raelan's eyes lingered on her just long enough to make her heart skip, but then he turned and walked toward the throne.

The crowd parted for him, their gazes reverent, their whispers hushed. As Raelan approached the steps to the dais, Kaela stepped out of the shadows, moving with purpose, her gaze locked on the crown resting on the velvet cushion beside the throne. The same crown that had been promised to him. The same crown that had been stolen from him.

And tonight, the same crown that would burn a hole through everything they had ever known.

But she wasn't the only one watching.

As Raelan reached the bottom of the steps, Kaela felt a presence behind her, sharp and unmistakable. She didn't have to turn to know who it was. She could feel him—his coldness, his determination. Roderick.

"Do you think you can stop this?" Roderick's voice was a whisper, a dangerous murmur that sent a chill crawling up her spine. He was standing only a few steps away, his figure hidden in the shadows like a specter, watching as Raelan ascended the dais. "Do you really think you can stop him from taking what's his?"

Kaela didn't respond immediately. She knew what Roderick was trying to do. He was trying to goad her into revealing her plans. But she wouldn't let him. She wouldn't let him make her doubt herself.

"I don't have to stop him," she said quietly, her eyes still fixed on Raelan. "I just have to make sure he knows what he's doing."

Roderick let out a low chuckle. "And what is it you think he's doing, Kaela? This is his birthright. You're not going to take that from him."

"No," Kaela replied, her voice steady. "But I'm going to make sure he knows the price of wearing that crown."

The room seemed to hold its breath as Raelan knelt before his uncle, King Alric, who stood at the top of the dais, the crown in his hands. The moment was electric. Kaela could feel the tension in the air, the weight of the centuries of history pressing down on them all.

King Alric's voice rang out, strong and clear. "Raelan, son of my brother, heir to the throne of Whitecliff, it is time for you to take your rightful place."

As Alric held the crown high above Raelan's head, Kaela moved without thinking, her steps quick and purposeful. She had no time to hesitate. She had no time to second-guess herself.

In a blur, she reached the edge of the dais, her hand reaching for the small dagger she kept hidden beneath her cloak. She was so close. So close to stopping this madness. Her eyes locked on the crown—the golden circle that would seal Raelan's fate.

But before she could act, a hand clamped down on her wrist.

"You're too late."

Roderick's grip tightened, and Kaela stumbled, her dagger falling from her grasp. She spun around, ready to strike, but he was already there—his body blocking her path, his dark eyes gleaming with malicious satisfaction.

"I told you," he whispered. "You don't understand. This is already over."

Kaela struggled against him, her muscles straining, but he was too strong. She could feel the heat of his breath on her neck, the coldness of his gaze seeping into her soul. He wasn't just here to stop her. He was here to ensure Raelan's coronation would be a coronation in blood.

With a twist, Kaela broke free, her hand flying to her waist where she kept another hidden knife. She had no choice now. There was no going back.

But Roderick was faster.

He grabbed her by the throat, his hand tight around her neck, and for a moment, Kaela's vision blurred. She gasped for breath, her hand clawing at his, trying to pry his fingers away. His grip tightened, and she felt her world slipping away from her.

Raelan's voice pierced through the chaos. "Let her go."

Kaela's heart stopped. She turned her head, barely able to focus, but she saw Raelan standing there, his body tense, his eyes hard as he looked at Roderick. His uncle had the crown in his hand, his gaze flicking between the two of them. For a moment, the room held its breath again, waiting for the prince to make his move.

Roderick didn't release her, his grip like iron. "This is none of your concern, Raelan."

But Raelan stepped forward, his voice calm, but filled with authority. "Let her go."

Roderick hesitated, his eyes flicking to the crown in Alric's hands, but then he released Kaela. She fell to the floor in a heap, gasping for air, but her gaze never left Raelan. She could feel the heat of his eyes, the tension in the air thickening with every passing second.

Raelan stood over her, his gaze unreadable, his hand outstretched as if he wanted to help her up. But Kaela didn't take it. She didn't need him. She didn't want him to have control over her anymore.

Roderick's lips curled into a sneer. "You're making a mistake, Raelan," he said quietly, his voice dripping with malice. "You can't just throw away everything you've worked for."

Raelan turned toward his uncle, his eyes cold. "I'm not throwing it away, Uncle. But I'm not going to let you control me, either."

Alric stepped forward, his voice booming in the silence. "Raelan, this is your moment. This is your chance to claim the throne."

Kaela's heart pounded in her chest as she watched the scene unfold before her. She could see the way Raelan's hands clenched into fists, the way his jaw tightened as if he was holding onto something—something deep inside him that was at war with everything around him.

And then, Raelan turned to face her. His gaze was filled with something she couldn't name, but it wasn't anger or resentment. It was… regret.

"Kaela," he said, his voice barely above a whisper.

And for one fleeting moment, everything seemed to stand still.

But the crown had already been placed on his head. And as Raelan stood there, crowned in gold, Kaela realized that the coronation was not just for the kingdom. It was for him, too. It was the final step in the long, painful journey of becoming something he could never undo.

A prince in name. A king in blood.

And nothing would ever be the same again.

Thirteen

The Betrayal of a Crown

The throne room was silent. The air was thick with anticipation, the kind that clung to every corner like smoke after a fire. Whitecliff had waited for this moment for ten long years—Raelan's return, his rise to power. And yet, as Kaela stood there, her heart racing in her chest, she couldn't shake the feeling that something was wrong.

Raelan sat on the throne now, his posture perfect, his crown gleaming in the flickering torchlight. He had the look of a king, but there was something in his eyes—something that betrayed the weight of the decision he had made. The crown was no longer a symbol of hope. It was a shackle.

The courtiers around her were still in their places, some whispering excitedly, others watching with quiet reverence. But Kaela couldn't see any of them. All she saw was him. Raelan, the man she had loved, now trapped by the crown he had fought so hard to reclaim. She had been in this room once before, standing beside him, believing that the future they had imagined was within reach. Now, it seemed that all of it had been a lie.

The doors to the throne room opened with a loud groan, and the sound of approaching footsteps brought Kaela's attention back to the present. She didn't have to look to know who it was. She could feel the weight of his presence before he even entered the room.

King Alric.

The man who had stolen Raelan's throne. The man who had crushed everything Raelan had stood for, and now, with a crown in his hands, had crowned his nephew to make his power even more secure.

Kaela's stomach twisted as Alric stepped forward, his eyes never leaving the throne. He was everything she had come to despise—cold, calculating, and manipulative. There was no love in his eyes, no warmth. Only the hunger for control, for dominance, for power.

Raelan's eyes flickered toward the king, and for a moment, Kaela saw the conflict in them. He wasn't the same man she had once known. There was no more fire in his gaze, no more of the rebellious spirit that had once burned so brightly. Now, there was only the weight of duty.

Alric smiled, his lips curling as he stepped toward the throne. "Raelan, my dear nephew. You have done well. You have accepted your place."

Raelan didn't respond. He merely stared ahead, the tension in his body palpable.

The moment stretched, and then Alric's voice broke the silence. "But do you understand what it means, Raelan? To wear this crown?" His gaze turned dark. "Do you understand the blood it demands?"

Kaela could see the muscles in Raelan's neck tighten, his jaw clenching. His hands rested on the arms of the throne, white knuckles betraying the battle waging inside him.

"I understand," Raelan said, his voice cold, clipped. "I've always understood."

But Alric's eyes gleamed with something darker, something Kaela couldn't place. He stepped closer to Raelan, his voice lowering.

"You understand the cost of loyalty, then?" Alric whispered, a sneer twisting his lips. "Because I have been loyal to you, Raelan. I have kept your name alive, even as you were hidden away. I have waited for the day you would return."

Raelan's eyes flickered with something—a flash of old resentment, perhaps, or the shadow of regret. But it was gone almost as quickly as it had appeared. His face remained impassive, his posture stiff.

"You are loyal to power, Alric," Kaela said, her voice cutting through the thick silence. She couldn't stop herself. It was as if the words had been building up inside her for years. "You've always been loyal to power, not to family."

Alric's eyes snapped to her, a cold gleam in them. "Ah, the thief speaks," he said, his voice dripping with mockery. "You should know, Kaela, that loyalty is the highest currency in this kingdom. And it is a price we all must pay."

She stepped forward, her eyes not leaving Raelan's. "No. Some of us still have the choice to walk away. Some of us still have a soul."

Raelan's gaze met hers, and for a brief moment, she saw it—the flicker of the man she had once known, the man who had been willing to burn the world to build something better. But it vanished before she could even breathe. He turned away, as if the brief connection they shared had never happened.

Alric smirked, clearly enjoying the exchange between them. "You see, Kaela, you've failed to understand the truth of the matter. This kingdom was never about you. It was never about Raelan."

Kaela's blood ran cold. "What do you mean?" she asked, her voice a mere rasp.

Alric's smile grew wider, a cruel gleam in his eyes. "I've always known what was required to rule," he said. "Raelan may have been born to the crown, but it was I who kept the kingdom from falling into chaos. It was I who made sure it survived."

He turned back to Raelan, who had remained eerily silent throughout the exchange, his gaze fixed on his uncle. "And now, it is time for you to understand the cost of your birthright. The crown will not just be given to you, Raelan. You will earn it."

Alric's hand rested on the back of Raelan's throne, a silent command. "And to earn it, you must prove your loyalty. Not just to me, but to the kingdom itself."

Raelan's face remained unreadable, but Kaela could see the muscles in his jaw twitch, the tension in his hands tightening as he gripped the arms of the throne.

"I'm ready," Raelan finally said, his voice hollow. "I've always been ready."

But Kaela could see it. She could see the hesitation in his eyes. He wasn't ready. No one could ever be ready for this.

Alric's gaze flickered to her, and his lips curled into a wicked grin. "You see, Kaela, I have given my nephew everything he has ever wanted. And now, the true test begins."

He stepped back from Raelan, his eyes dark with intent. "Your loyalty will be tested, Raelan. In ways you can't even imagine."

Raelan's eyes flickered with uncertainty, but he didn't speak. He couldn't, not now. Not in front of the court, not in front of Alric, not when every eye in the room was upon him, waiting for his next move.

And then, without warning, Alric gestured toward the door.

"Bring him."

A figure stepped forward, shrouded in darkness, from the shadows beyond the throne room. It was a man, his face hidden beneath a dark cloak, his steps slow, deliberate.

"Who is this?" Raelan demanded, his voice rising.

Alric's smile widened as the figure stepped into the torchlight, revealing his face.

Kaela's breath caught in her throat.

The man before them was none other than Captain Aldric—the same man who had once sworn loyalty to Raelan's father, the same man who had betrayed them all.

"What is this, Uncle?" Raelan's voice was a harsh whisper. "You would bring him before me?"

Alric turned to face Raelan, his eyes cold. "I had no choice, nephew. There are those who would see you fail. There are those who would see the crown slip from your grasp."

He looked back at Aldric, who stood silently, his posture rigid, his eyes like a predator watching its prey. "Aldric knows what must be done."

Raelan's face drained of color as the weight of Alric's words sunk in. "You… you want me to kill him," he whispered, the words barely escaping his lips.

Alric's smile was dark, sinister. "Not kill, nephew. Prove. Prove to me that you have the strength to wear the crown."

Kaela watched in horror as Raelan's eyes flickered between his uncle and the man who had once been his protector. Aldric stood still, as if resigned to his fate, but there was no mercy in his eyes.

Raelan's fingers clenched on the throne, the muscles in his arms straining. "No… I won't do this."

Alric's expression hardened. "You will. Because if you don't, you'll lose everything. Everything."

The room fell into an eerie silence as Raelan stood there, torn between the weight of his bloodline and the man he had once been. Kaela could see it—the battle raging inside him, the tug of loyalty to his uncle, to his kingdom, and the echoes of the man who had fought so hard to reclaim his throne.

But there was no turning back now. Raelan's eyes shifted to Aldric, then back to Alric. His shoulders slumped, and with a heavy sigh, he rose from the throne.

"I will prove myself."

The room was silent as he made his way toward Aldric, the crown still sitting heavy on his head. Raelan reached for the sword at his side, his hand trembling slightly as he drew the blade. He faced Aldric with grim resolve, the court watching in hushed silence.

"Do it," Alric's voice rang out.

Raelan hesitated for a brief moment, his gaze flickering toward Kaela. And in that moment, everything seemed to stop—the weight of the kingdom, the crown, the betrayal—all of it hung in the air like a silent, oppressive force.

But in the end, it wasn't the crown that weighed most on Raelan. It was the choice that would define him.

And as his sword rose, Kaela understood—the prince she had once known was gone, and in his place stood a king who had already betrayed everything for the crown.

A Kingdom in Flames

The castle trembled beneath Kaela's feet, its foundations shaking with the fury of battle. She could hear the sounds of war outside—the clash of steel on steel, the cries of men falling to the ground, and the roar of the flames licking at the castle's walls.

Her heart was pounding in her chest, her hands slick with sweat as she moved through the corridors. The path ahead was filled with chaos, but there was no turning back now. Raelan's decision to wear the crown had set this course in motion, and now the very kingdom he had fought to reclaim was unraveling before their eyes.

Raelan stood at the top of the stairs, his silhouette a dark shadow against the flickering light of the torches. His armor gleamed, but the crown on his head was a heavy weight, not a symbol of glory but of something darker, more dangerous.

Kaela had watched as the first flames spread across the castle grounds, consuming the wooden structures outside the walls. But it wasn't just the fire. It was the rebellion—like an unshackled beast, it had surged forward with a speed that even Raelan couldn't have anticipated. His uncle's supporters, the very men who had placed him on the throne, had turned against him, their loyalty now crumbling under the pressure of the battle.

Raelan's eyes flicked toward her as she approached, his gaze haunted, filled with the weight of the crown and what it had cost him. She could see it in the tight set of his shoulders, in the way his hands clenched around the hilt of his sword.

"I didn't want this," Raelan said, his voice heavy with regret. "I didn't want any of this."

Kaela's heart ached, but she didn't allow herself to feel sympathy. She couldn't. Not now. Not when the world was crumbling around them. The kingdom they had both dreamed of—fought for—was burning.

"Then why did you take it?" she asked, her voice sharp, cutting through the tension between them.

Raelan turned away, his eyes focused on the chaos outside, the screams of men and women waging a war that had no victors. "Because I thought I could save it. I thought I could rebuild everything. But I was wrong."

The wind howled through the broken windows of the great hall, sending bits of dust and debris swirling through the air. It was a cold reminder that there was no escaping the reality they had found themselves in. There was no escaping the price of the crown, the price of ambition.

"I thought you were different," Kaela said, her words laced with bitterness. "I thought you had a chance to be the man who could change all of this. But you chose him."

Raelan flinched at her words, and for a brief moment, Kaela saw the man he had once been—the prince who had stood beside her, the man she had loved. But it was fleeting, lost in the chaos of the fire and the blood that now stained their hands.

"I thought I could make things right," Raelan whispered, his voice raw. "But I don't know what's left to save."

Before Kaela could respond, the doors to the hall slammed open with a deafening crash. The figure that stepped through was not one she had expected—Roderick, his face a mask of fury, his cloak trailing behind him like a storm.

"The kingdom is burning, Raelan," Roderick said, his voice low, cold. "And you're sitting here, wallowing in your failure. You should have known this would happen."

Raelan's face twisted in anger. "This is your doing, Roderick," he spat, his hands tightening around his sword. "You're the one who manipulated me. You're the one who played me like a fool."

Roderick's lips curled into a dark smile. "I didn't play you, Raelan. You played yourself. You wanted this. You wanted the crown. And now you've got it. But you don't know how to wear it."

Kaela stepped forward, her voice cutting through the tension. "Enough, both of you. This isn't helping."

Roderick's eyes flicked to her, and for a moment, there was something in his gaze—something dangerous and hungry. He didn't answer her, but his gaze lingered, like a predator sizing up its prey.

"The castle's walls are already crumbling, Raelan," Roderick continued, his voice dark and menacing. "The rebellion is gaining ground. You may have the crown, but you'll never have the loyalty. Not anymore."

Raelan turned toward him, his expression hardening. "I'll fight for this kingdom. I'll fight for what's mine."

Roderick chuckled darkly. "You think you still have the power to fight, Raelan? You've already lost." He stepped closer, his voice dropping to a whisper. "You just don't know it yet."

Kaela watched, her heart heavy with the weight of the choice she had to make. She had come here to stop Raelan from destroying himself, but she had failed. The fire had spread too far, the blood had already been spilled. There was no going back.

The battle was raging outside, but the real fight—the one that would determine the future of Whitecliff—was happening right here, in this very room.

"You don't understand, Roderick," Raelan said, his voice low but firm. "I'm not like you. I don't need to play games. I'll destroy anyone who stands in my way."

Roderick's eyes glittered with amusement. "You think you can destroy me? You're nothing without me, Raelan. You always were."

Kaela's hands clenched into fists, her mind racing. "Stop," she said, her voice shaking with a fury she could no longer control. "Stop this madness, both of you. This is exactly what they want. This war, this chaos—it's all a game to them."

Raelan and Roderick turned to her, their expressions darkening. "What do you mean?" Raelan asked, his voice low, confused.

Kaela took a deep breath, forcing herself to stay calm. "The rebellion isn't just about taking the throne. It's about everything—the blood, the power, the destruction. They want this to burn. They want us all to burn."

Raelan's eyes widened, the realization dawning on him. "You're saying that this isn't just about me and my uncle?"

"No," Kaela said, her voice steady. "It's about control. It's about tearing this kingdom apart so that nothing is left but ashes. They want to rule over nothing. They want to watch it all burn."

Roderick's lips twisted into a smirk. "And you think you can stop it, Kaela? You think you can stop me?"

Kaela didn't answer him. She couldn't. Not when everything they had ever known was falling apart. She turned to Raelan, her eyes pleading. "You can stop this, Raelan. You can make a choice. You can end this war before it destroys everything."

Raelan stood still, his expression unreadable. The fire outside had reached the castle gates now, the sound of the flames rising as if they, too, were alive, hungering for more.

"I can't," he whispered, the weight of his words sinking deep into Kaela's soul. "I can't stop it. I've already made my choice. I've already sealed my fate."

The ground shook beneath their feet, the sound of the distant battle echoing in the distance. The rebellion was closing in.

"I've already lost," Raelan whispered, more to himself than anyone else.

Kaela's heart cracked. The man she had once loved was gone, replaced by a king who had traded everything for power.

"You haven't lost yet," Kaela said, her voice barely above a whisper. "But if you don't make a choice, you will."

Roderick laughed, the sound like a knife to Kaela's heart. "This is the end, Raelan. You've already made your choice. It's too late to go back now."

Raelan's eyes shifted to Kaela, his gaze haunted, his body stiff with the weight of his decisions. His fingers tightened around the hilt of his sword.

For a moment, it seemed as though he might fight. He might rise against it all, against the destruction, against the fire, and the blood.

But then, he turned away from Kaela, his shoulders slumped, his sword still at his side. He walked toward the windows, his back to them all, the weight of his crown now unbearable.

Kaela's breath caught in her throat. "Raelan—"

But it was too late.

The castle walls shook again. This time, it wasn't just the rumble of distant battle. This was something more. The fire had reached the gates. The rebellion was at the castle doors.

Raelan's voice was barely audible above the chaos that now surrounded them. "It's too late. Whitecliff is already lost."

And as the flames reached the castle, the weight of his words struck like a final blow, and Kaela knew—the kingdom was already in flames.

Fifteen

A Love That Cannot Be

The sky above Whitecliff was the color of bruised shadows, a deep, unsettling purple as if it too knew the pain of what had happened beneath its expanse. The city was burning. The towers of the castle rose like jagged teeth, silhouetted against the flickering light of the distant flames. There was no escaping the chaos now. No place to hide from the consequences of Raelan's choices.

Kaela stood at the edge of the balcony, her back straight, her hands gripping the stone so tightly that her knuckles were white. The wind howled, carrying the acrid scent of smoke through the air. Below, the city was alive with movement—guards rushing to defend what remained, courtiers scrambling for safety, and the rebels, like shadows in the night, closing in on the final remnants of the kingdom's heart.

Her heart pounded in her chest, the rhythm echoing in her ears, drowning out the sounds of the dying city. She had never felt so far from everything she had known. The life she had built, the dreams she had held close, had all crumbled to dust in the span of a single decision. Raelan's decision.

Raelan.

She had loved him once, with everything she had. The young prince who had promised her a future, a life together—away from the shadows. The man who had once burned with rebellion, with the fire to change the world. But now, that fire was gone, replaced by the cold, indifferent man who wore the crown of a kingdom that no longer existed.

Kaela closed her eyes, the sting of her own tears pressing against her eyelids, but she refused to let them fall. She couldn't afford the weakness. She had made her choice, too.

The door behind her creaked open, but she didn't turn around. She didn't need to. She knew who it was. The sound of footsteps was unmistakable—the heavy tread of someone who had no fear of what was coming. Raelan.

He didn't speak at first, but Kaela could feel him standing there, just behind her, his presence like a shadow that clung to every inch of her being. She took a deep breath, her gaze still fixed on the burning city below. She couldn't face him. Not yet. Not after everything.

"I thought you were gone," Raelan's voice was soft, hesitant, like the man she had once known was fighting to break free from the shell that had encased him.

Kaela didn't look at him, her fingers trembling as she continued to grip the stone. "I was. But you called me back." The bitterness in her voice wasn't something she could hide.

There was silence behind her, and she could almost hear the way Raelan's thoughts raced, the uncertainty, the confusion. She knew him well enough to know that he was never certain of his next move—at least not anymore.

"Kaela," he said her name as if it were the only thing left in the world he could hold onto.

She felt his presence before she felt his touch. It was light at first—his hand resting on the railing beside hers, close but not quite touching. The space between them was like a chasm, wide and impossible to bridge.

She turned her head slightly, just enough to meet his gaze. His eyes were hollow, as if he had already lost everything, and there was nothing left to fight for. But the pain in them, the weight of his choices—it was all still there, a burden that was slowly suffocating him.

"I don't understand why you're still here," he whispered, his voice hoarse. "You should hate me. I've made everything worse. I've ruined everything."

Kaela's lips parted, but no words came out at first. How could she explain what she felt? How could she put the anguish of watching him slip further and further from who he once was into words? The man she had loved was dead, replaced by someone who no longer knew who he was.

"You don't get to do this, Raelan," she said finally, her voice cracking with the weight of her own emotions. "You don't get to stand here and feel sorry for yourself. You don't get to make me your excuse for what's happening to Whitecliff. You chose this. You chose the crown over everything."

Raelan flinched as if her words struck harder than any sword could. He stepped back slightly, like he couldn't bear to hear her truth.

"I didn't want this," he said quietly, his voice almost a whisper. "I never wanted the crown. I never wanted this kingdom to fall into chaos."

Kaela laughed bitterly, the sound echoing in the hollow of the room. "Then why did you take it?" she asked. "Why did you put it on? Why did you make the choice to become this—a man who doesn't know how to walk away from the blood he's spilled, the lives he's destroyed?"

Raelan's face twisted, pain flashing across his features. He didn't answer her. He couldn't.

She didn't give him time to respond. "You were never supposed to be like this," she whispered, her words lost in the breeze that blew across the balcony. "You were supposed to be the one who broke the chains. But instead, you're wearing them willingly."

Raelan stepped forward again, his voice low and raw. "I didn't want this, Kaela. I didn't want to hurt anyone." His hand reached out, brushing against her arm, but she pulled away, the sting of his touch burning deeper than she expected.

She looked at him then, truly looked at him, seeing the man he had become, and the man he had been, and realized that there was no going back. There had never been any going back.

"I don't know who you are anymore," she said, her voice breaking, but her resolve unyielding. "The man I loved is gone."

Raelan's breath hitched, and for a moment, Kaela thought she saw the flicker of something—something raw, something real— but it disappeared as quickly as it came.

"I never meant to become this," he whispered. "But I did. And I can't undo it. I can't undo any of it, Kaela."

The sound of chaos from below grew louder, and she knew the rebellion had breached the castle walls. It was too late for Whitecliff. Too late for any of them. The kingdom was already slipping into ruin, and Raelan had made his choice.

"You can still stop this," Kaela said, her voice growing desperate. "You can stop the bloodshed. You can turn your back on everything you've done and walk away. For once, choose something different. You can still—"

Raelan shook his head slowly, his eyes never leaving hers. "I can't. I've already chosen." His gaze shifted to the city below, the flames licking at the night sky. "This is the price of a crown, Kaela. And I don't know how to make it stop."

For a moment, Kaela stood there, staring at the man who had once been her everything. He was broken. Lost. And the kingdom around them, the dreams they had shared, had turned to ash.

She closed her eyes, tears she hadn't known she'd been holding back finally slipping down her cheeks. But she didn't let them fall. She didn't have time for that now.

The sound of a distant crash echoed through the night, followed by a roar of flames. The city was crumbling, the castle was crumbling, and everything they had ever fought for was being swallowed whole by the fire.

"I'm sorry, Kaela," Raelan said softly, his voice filled with a sadness that twisted her insides. "I never meant for it to end like this."

She shook her head, the tears finally falling as she stepped back from him, her heart breaking in ways she couldn't explain.

"I know," she whispered, her voice hoarse with the weight of it all. "But it has to end. It has to."

Raelan reached out to her one last time, his hand trembling, but Kaela stepped back, shaking her head as she wiped the tears away.

"This love…" she whispered, her words filled with pain and acceptance. "It was never meant to be."

Raelan's face crumpled with regret, but she didn't wait for him to speak again. She turned and walked away, her steps slow but purposeful. The sound of the flames and the cries of the dying filled her ears, but it was the silence in her heart that kept her moving forward.

There was no turning back now. There was no love to save them. The fire had already claimed everything.

And in its wake, there would be nothing left but the ashes of a kingdom, and the shadow of a love that could never be.

Sixteen

The Queen's Last Move

The castle was a ruin.

Kaela could feel the weight of its crumbling walls around her as she walked through the shattered corridors, her footsteps echoing in the silence that had replaced the once vibrant halls. The air was thick with smoke, the scent of burnt wood and dying embers curling around her like an oppressive blanket. The distant cries of the wounded and dying rose like a mournful choir, but they couldn't reach her now. Not here. Not where she needed to be.

She had been prepared for this, but the sight of it—the devastation—was something she hadn't anticipated. Whitecliff was falling apart. The rebellion had breached the castle walls and now, the heart of the kingdom was being torn to pieces by the very people Raelan had sworn to protect.

Her heart ached for him, but she wouldn't allow herself to stop. She couldn't. Not when the real battle was yet to come.

The throne room loomed before her, its once grand double doors now hanging at odd angles, the wood cracked and scorched from the fire. She didn't hesitate. With a swift motion, she pushed the door open, her hand steady despite the adrenaline surging through her veins. The room inside was just as she had imagined—ruined, soaked in the blood of battle. But it wasn't the blood of soldiers that stained the floor. It was the blood of a queen.

Standing at the far end of the throne room, the woman who had once ruled this kingdom with such ruthless precision was now a figure of sorrow. Queen Evelyne, Raelan's betrothed, stood before the throne, her head held high despite the streaks of dirt and blood that marred her once immaculate attire.

Kaela's breath caught in her throat as she watched Evelyne. The woman's beauty, once a thing of legend, now seemed as hollow as the kingdom itself. There was a coldness to her gaze, something calculating and detached. But behind it, there was something else—a deep, unspoken sadness, as though she too understood the inevitable end that had come for them all.

"You're too late," Evelyne's voice was like ice, cutting through the stillness of the room.

Kaela didn't flinch. She had expected this. Expected the queen's words to be laced with venom, with fury. But instead, there was something almost resigned about her tone, as if she had already accepted the truth of what was happening.

"Am I?" Kaela replied, her voice steady, but the weight of it hung between them. The room felt smaller now, as if the walls were closing in around them. There was no room for hesitation, no space for pity.

Evelyne turned her head, her piercing green eyes narrowing as they met Kaela's. For a moment, the two women simply stared at each other, and Kaela saw it—the understanding in Evelyne's gaze. She wasn't just the queen now. She wasn't just a woman fighting to hold onto a lost kingdom. She was something else. Something far more dangerous.

"You think you've won," Evelyne said, her lips curling into a bitter smile. "But the game isn't over yet."

Kaela took a step forward, her heart pounding in her chest. "What do you mean?"

Evelyne's expression darkened. "You don't know what's at stake, Kaela. You never did. Raelan thought he could change the world, but he was always too naive. He never understood the cost of power."

"I'm not here to discuss Raelan's mistakes," Kaela replied, her voice cutting through the queen's venom. "I'm here to end this madness. To end your game."

Evelyne laughed bitterly, the sound echoing off the stone walls. "End it? You can't end what's already been set in motion. You think you can save this kingdom? You think you can save Raelan? You think anyone can?"

Kaela's heart skipped a beat at the mention of his name. She knew what Evelyne was trying to do—bait her, provoke her. But Kaela wasn't falling for it. Not now. Not when everything was about to come to a head.

"I'm not here to save anyone," Kaela said, her voice low but filled with a cold certainty. "I'm here to make sure you don't destroy any more lives."

Evelyne's eyes flared with anger, and for a moment, Kaela thought the queen might strike at her, might give in to the rage that had been festering inside her for so long. But then, something shifted in Evelyne's expression. The anger faded, replaced by something deeper, something more calculating.

"Do you think you can defeat me, Kaela?" she asked, her voice now laced with a quiet malice. "I've been playing this game long before you ever stepped foot in Whitecliff. You have no idea what you're up against."

Kaela didn't respond at first. She couldn't. The weight of Evelyne's words lingered in the air, and for the briefest of moments, she wondered if maybe she had miscalculated. Maybe she didn't understand the true depths of the queen's power, the extent of her ruthlessness.

But then she remembered the destruction outside, the rebellion that had ravaged the streets, the bodies that lay in the halls of the castle. Raelan had been a fool. Evelyne was not just a woman scorned. She was a force of nature, a woman who had learned how to survive at any cost.

Kaela clenched her fists. She had come too far to turn back now.

"What is it you want, Evelyne?" Kaela's voice was steady, her gaze unyielding. "What is it that you think you can still control?"

Evelyne took a step forward, her gaze never leaving Kaela's. "What I want is to make sure that this kingdom remains mine. That nothing changes. Not even you."

The words hit Kaela like a physical blow. She had always known that Evelyne was dangerous, but she had never truly understood the depth of the queen's madness until now. She wasn't just trying to keep her position. She was trying to keep control over everything—even if it meant burning Whitecliff to the ground.

"What did you do?" Kaela's voice trembled, the realization dawning on her. "What have you done to the city?"

Evelyne's lips curled into a smile. "You think Raelan could change anything? You think he could have saved this kingdom?" She laughed bitterly. "No, Kaela. You've all been pawns in a game I've been playing for years. And now that the pieces are in place, the game is over. I've already won."

Kaela took a step back, her mind racing, the weight of the

queen's words sinking in like a leaden weight. The rebellion, the chaos—it had all been part of the plan. Evelyne had known this would happen. She had orchestrated it, set it all in motion to destroy Raelan, to destroy everything he had fought for.

"You killed this kingdom," Kaela said, her voice hoarse with disbelief. "You killed everything he believed in."

Evelyne's smile widened. "I did what had to be done. Raelan was never meant to be king. He was always a fool, just like his father. And now, the throne is mine."

Kaela's blood ran cold. "You think you can just take it?" she spat. "That you can just burn everything down and call it yours?"

Evelyne stepped closer, her voice a soft whisper in Kaela's ear. "I already have. And I'm not going to stop. Not until everything Raelan built is gone."

The door to the throne room creaked open then, and the sound of heavy footsteps echoed in the distance. Kaela turned sharply, her hand reaching for the hilt of her dagger, but Evelyne was already there, her hand outstretched, her fingers curled like claws.

"I wouldn't be so quick to make a move, Kaela," Evelyne said, her voice dark with warning. "You're not the only one with power here."

Kaela's breath caught in her throat as the figure stepped into the room, the figure she had feared would appear—the figure she had known would come to claim what was rightfully his.

Raelan stood in the doorway, his expression unreadable, his hands clenched at his sides. The weight of the crown on his head was almost suffocating, the golden band that had once been a symbol of his birthright now a symbol of his failure. His eyes flicked between Kaela and Evelyne, and for a moment, he seemed lost, uncertain of what to do, of where to go.

"Raelan," Kaela whispered, her voice trembling. "You don't have to do this."

He looked at her, and for a moment, there was something in his eyes—something she couldn't place. But then, just as quickly as it had come, it was gone.

"I don't have a choice, Kaela," he said softly, his voice thick with regret. "I never did."

Evelyne stepped forward, her hand reaching out to him, her fingers brushing his arm. "You never did," she echoed, her voice like silk. "But now, the kingdom is mine. You're mine."

Raelan's eyes flickered between the two women, the weight of the crown on his head almost unbearable.

Kaela could feel it then—the final blow. Raelan wasn't just lost to her. He had already chosen. And now, the kingdom, the future, everything they had fought for—was nothing more than dust in the wind.

In the end, it was the queen who had won.

Seventeen

The Final Confrontation

T he wind howled through the broken windows, carrying with it the scent of ash and destruction. Outside, Whitecliff burned—its streets filled with chaos, the cries of the wounded and the dying rising to meet the heavens, but inside the castle, there was an eerie silence. The air was heavy, thick with the weight of choices that could never be undone. The walls of the throne room, once magnificent, now stood as the crumbling remnants of a kingdom falling apart.

Kaela stood in the center of the room, her gaze fixed on the throne before her. The golden seat, meant to represent power and royalty, now felt like an empty monument to lost dreams. Raelan had been seated there not long ago, his eyes haunted, the crown heavy on his head. But now, it was as if he had never truly belonged. The power that had once called to him was gone, smothered by the weight of his own choices.

The room felt suffocating, and every part of Kaela screamed to leave, to run far from this madness, but her feet wouldn't move. She was trapped, not just in the room, but in everything that had led her here. The battle outside, the kingdom crumbling, Raelan's surrender to his uncle—everything had led to this one moment. She had tried to stop it, tried to make him see, but now the inevitable had arrived.

The throne room doors creaked open, and Kaela's heart skipped a beat. She didn't have to turn around to know who was standing there. She could feel his presence—the weight of him pressing against her back, the shadows that seemed to gather around him like a storm. Raelan.

Her chest tightened, but she forced herself to stand still, to face the reality she had been avoiding. He was here, but was he the man she had once known? Or had he already given up everything for a crown that wasn't his to claim?

Raelan didn't speak at first. He stood in the doorway, his posture rigid, his eyes studying her as if she were a puzzle he could no longer solve. The crown sat heavy on his head, the weight of it dragging him down in a way Kaela had never seen before. He looked like a man who had been consumed by something darker, something he could not outrun.

"You should leave," Kaela said, her voice steady despite the storm inside her. "There's nothing left for you here."

Raelan's eyes flicked to her, but he didn't respond. His gaze shifted to the throne, then back to Kaela. The words were there, she could see it in the tension of his shoulders, in the way his hands clenched at his sides.

"I thought I could fix this," he finally said, his voice low, like a confession. "I thought I could save Whitecliff. But I was wrong."

Kaela's breath caught in her throat, but she didn't speak. She couldn't. What was there to say? Raelan's confession only confirmed what she had known for so long. He wasn't the man he had once been. The fire that had burned inside him was gone, and in its place, there was only regret and exhaustion.

"The kingdom is already lost," Kaela said softly, her voice filled with sorrow. "It doesn't matter what you do now. There's no way back."

Raelan took a step forward, his eyes dark with a mixture of rage and despair. "You think I don't know that?" he snapped, his voice rising. "You think I wanted any of this to happen? I never asked for this crown, Kaela. It was forced on me."

"I know," she replied, the words bitter in her mouth. "But you wore it willingly. You chose it. And now, this kingdom is paying the price."

Raelan flinched, as though her words had struck a nerve. But he didn't look away. His eyes were filled with something— something she couldn't place. He opened his mouth to speak, but before he could, the sound of footsteps interrupted him.

A shadow moved at the far end of the throne room, and Kaela's heart sank. The unmistakable silhouette of King Alric appeared in the doorway, his cloak trailing behind him like a dark cloud. His eyes were cold, calculating, as they moved between Raelan and Kaela.

"Father…" Raelan's voice broke with the word, a mixture of confusion and anger. "You did this. You pushed me into this. You wanted me to wear the crown, and now look at what's happened."

Alric didn't flinch. His expression remained as icy as ever, his presence like a force of nature that would not be denied. "You were always too weak, Raelan," he said quietly, his voice as smooth as silk. "You never understood what it takes to rule. You never understood the price of power."

Raelan's hands clenched into fists, his jaw tight. "And you? You think you understand power, Father? You think you can control everything? You've destroyed everything, and now you expect me to clean up the mess you've made?"

Alric's eyes gleamed with cold amusement. "I've done what was necessary to ensure the survival of Whitecliff. You may not understand it now, but you will. You will thank me one day for what I've done."

Kaela's breath quickened. "You're wrong, Alric," she said, her voice shaking with anger. "You're the one who's destroyed this kingdom. You've twisted everything, used Raelan as your pawn, and now you want to blame him for the consequences."

Alric turned his gaze to her, and for a moment, she saw the slightest flicker of disdain in his eyes. "You should know your place, Kaela. You've been nothing but a distraction from the moment you arrived. You think you can change this? You think you can undo what's been done?"

Before Kaela could respond, the sound of heavy boots echoed in the hallway. The doors to the throne room slammed open, and several guards rushed inside, their swords drawn, their faces stern.

"Father," one of them said, his voice sharp. "The rebellion has reached the outer walls. They're breaking through."

Kaela's heart skipped a beat. The rebellion was at their doorstep. The kingdom was already on the verge of collapse, and now, the walls were literally crumbling around them.

Raelan turned to his father, his eyes filled with a mixture of anger and helplessness. "What are we going to do?"

Alric's expression remained impassive, but there was a glint in his eyes that Kaela didn't trust. "We will fight," he said coldly. "We will defend Whitecliff. We will not let it fall."

"You can't fight this, Father," Raelan said, his voice strained. "You can't hold onto power when the people are already rising against you."

Alric's lips curled into a smile, but it was not one of reassurance. It was a smile that spoke of something darker. "It's not about holding onto power, Raelan. It's about crushing anyone who dares to stand against me."

Kaela stepped forward, her heart pounding in her chest. "You're willing to destroy everything, aren't you? You're willing to burn the kingdom to the ground just to keep your crown?"

Alric's gaze snapped to her, his eyes narrowing. "You've always been a thorn in my side, Kaela. Always questioning. Always challenging. But you don't understand. I'll do whatever it takes to keep Whitecliff standing. Even if it means you're burned along with it."

Raelan's eyes widened, and for the first time, Kaela saw something like fear in his expression. "Father, stop. Please."

But Alric wasn't listening. He turned toward the guards, his voice cold. "Ready the forces. We fight to the last man. Whitecliff will not fall."

As the guards filed out of the room, Kaela could see Raelan's face twisting with a mixture of disbelief and guilt. He had wanted to change things. He had wanted to be a king who led with honor. But now, he was trapped in a game he had never truly understood.

Raelan turned toward his father, his fists clenched. "I can't do this anymore, Father. I can't be your puppet."

Alric's expression darkened. "You don't have a choice, Raelan. You never did."

Kaela stepped forward, her voice rising with an urgency she couldn't suppress. "Raelan, listen to me. You don't have to do this. You don't have to follow him. You can still choose who you want to be."

Raelan's eyes flickered to hers, but there was a flicker of doubt, of something else, buried beneath the surface. "I don't know if I can stop it," he whispered.

Kaela took a step closer, her heart racing. "You still have a choice. You can fight for something better."

Raelan stood frozen, his eyes locked on hers, as if the weight of her words was the only thing keeping him grounded in this madness. And then, slowly, almost imperceptibly, he nodded.

But it wasn't enough. It wasn't enough to stop his father. It wasn't enough to stop the kingdom from burning.

Alric's voice broke through the tension. "Enough," he said coldly. "This charade is over."

With a wave of his hand, the guards returned, and Kaela knew then—the final confrontation was upon them. There was no more room for words, no more room for hope.

Only blood.

Eighteen

A Throne Restored

The flames outside were the first sign of the chaos that was about to unfold within the walls of Whitecliff's heart. The air was thick with the acrid scent of smoke, but even as the kingdom burned, the sound of clashing swords and the wails of the dying became a distant echo in Kaela's ears. Inside the castle, beneath the vaulted ceilings of the throne room, there was only silence. A heavy, suffocating silence that hung like a storm cloud before the downpour.

Kaela stood in the center of the room, her back straight, her eyes fixed on the throne that sat waiting before her—waiting for someone to claim it. Raelan had been standing there not long ago, wearing the crown like a heavy burden, his hands trembling as he had looked toward the city in ruin. Now, he was gone.

The door to the throne room creaked open behind her, the sound of boots on the stone floor growing louder. She didn't need to turn around to know who it was. She could feel his presence like a chill in the air—cold, calculating, a weight in the room that was impossible to ignore. King Alric.

He stepped into the room, his silhouette sharp against the flickering light of the nearby torches. His cloak swirled behind him, and as he walked toward the throne, the sound of his boots echoed in the silence. For a moment, Kaela thought he might just sit, claim the seat that had belonged to his brother before it had been torn from him. But he didn't. Instead, he paused, just out of reach of the throne, his eyes dark with something more than just ambition.

"You're too late," Kaela whispered, her voice breaking through the stillness. She hadn't realized how badly she had needed to say those words until they left her mouth. The final truth. The kingdom was already lost.

Alric's gaze flicked toward her, his eyes narrowing. "You think I'm here to claim the throne?" he asked, his voice low, dark. "I've had that throne for years, Kaela. This is not about a seat. This is about securing the future of Whitecliff. And you? You are just another casualty in this game."

Kaela didn't flinch. She had come too far to flinch now. Her heart was already broken—broken by Raelan's choices, broken by the cost of power and loyalty. The last remnants of hope she had clung to had shattered when she had realized that Raelan had never been able to choose. He had always been a pawn, just like everyone else.

"You're wrong, Alric," she said, her voice steady despite the cold rage bubbling beneath the surface. "This isn't about securing the kingdom. This is about you holding onto a crown that never should have been yours."

Alric smiled, that same cruel smile that had haunted her since the moment she had first set foot in Whitecliff. "You don't understand, do you?" he said softly, his gaze fixed on her. "You never did. The kingdom doesn't belong to Raelan. It belongs to whoever has the strength to take it. And now, it's mine again."

Kaela's pulse quickened. She knew what he was about to do. She could feel it in the air. He was going to make the final move. The game was over.

"Raelan will never rule again," Alric continued, his eyes glittering with something dark and triumphant. "He was weak, Kaela. A dreamer. You were right about one thing—he couldn't fight for the kingdom. But I can. I will."

And with that, Alric turned, his gaze fixed on the empty throne before him. He walked toward it, his steps slow, deliberate, and Kaela knew it was happening. He was going to take what had never truly belonged to him in the first place.

Kaela's heart sank. She could feel the weight of the crown that still sat on Raelan's head. She could feel it pressing down on her, pressing down on everything they had ever fought for. Raelan had believed in something better. But now, Alric's hands were closing in, ready to take it all.

Before she could stop herself, she lunged forward, her feet carrying her across the stone floor, her hands raised. "No!" she cried, her voice raw with the desperation of everything she had lost. "You don't deserve it! You never did!"

But Alric didn't turn around. He just kept walking, his eyes locked on the throne, his hands reaching for it.

"Enough," Alric said, his voice low, but commanding. He turned, his gaze sharp as he looked at Kaela. "It's already done. You can't change anything now."

The room seemed to close in around her, the walls pressing tighter, suffocating her with the reality of what was about to happen. Alric was going to sit on the throne, and once he did, there would be no going back. The kingdom would fall into his hands. Whitecliff would become his empire of ashes.

Kaela didn't have a choice. She was too far in now. There was no more running, no more hiding.

In that moment, she understood something that had been eluding her since the beginning. The kingdom—Whitecliff—wasn't about Raelan. It had never been. It had always been about power. And it wasn't hers to claim.

Before she could think, before she could even process what was happening, she moved.

She lunged at Alric, her body driven by instinct, her dagger slipping free from its sheath.

But Alric was faster.

He spun, his hand coming up to grab her wrist before she could strike, his grip like iron, crushing her arm with a single motion. Kaela gasped in pain, but she didn't stop. She twisted, pulling herself free from his grip, the dagger flashing as it found its mark.

Alric staggered back, his face contorted in rage, a low growl rumbling in his chest. His hand shot to his side, where a deep red stain bloomed across his tunic. Kaela's breath came in shallow gasps, her heart racing, but she didn't have time to enjoy the moment of victory.

Alric's eyes blazed with fury as he took a step back, drawing a sword from his side. "You think you can stop me, Kaela?" he hissed, his voice like gravel. "You think you can change the world with a blade?"

Kaela held her ground, her breath shaky but steady. "I'm not trying to change the world," she said, her voice low and determined. "I'm just trying to stop you from destroying it."

Alric raised his sword, his eyes narrowing as he advanced on her. "You can't defeat me, Kaela. I've already won."

Kaela's pulse quickened, but she didn't move. She could feel the weight of her own decision pressing on her chest, but there was no turning back now. She was going to fight for everything that had been stolen. She wasn't going to let him win.

But before they could clash, a sudden, sharp sound pierced the tension in the room—a cry from the door.

Raelan.

Kaela's heart stopped in her chest as the door to the throne room slammed open, and Raelan stepped into the room. His eyes locked on hers, filled with something raw, something unspoken. For a moment, it felt as though time stopped, as if the entire kingdom had ceased to exist.

Raelan's eyes flickered between Kaela and Alric, and in that instant, Kaela saw it—the man who had once been driven by rebellion, by hope, by the will to fight. But that man was gone. What stood before her now was a shadow—a man who had been broken, a king who had been crushed beneath the weight of his own choices.

"You don't have to do this, Raelan," Kaela said softly, her voice trembling. She wanted to believe that there was still a part of him left—the man she had loved, the man who had dreamed of a better future. But she didn't know if that man was still inside him.

Raelan's eyes flickered toward Alric, his father. And in that moment, Kaela saw the agony in his eyes, the confusion, the betrayal. But he didn't move. He didn't reach for the sword that hung at his side. Instead, his gaze shifted back to her, and the pain that had once been there was replaced by something colder.

"I've already made my choice," Raelan said, his voice hollow, broken. "I can't go back."

Kaela's heart shattered. "Raelan… please…"

But it was too late.

With a swift motion, Raelan turned, and before Kaela could react, he reached for the crown that still lay upon the throne. He lifted it slowly, his hands trembling as the weight of it seemed to consume him.

And in that moment, Kaela knew. The throne was his. It always had been. But the man she had once known was gone. He had become everything he had feared. The crown was restored, but at the cost of his soul.

Raelan placed the crown upon his head, and in that moment, Whitecliff died a little more. The throne was his. But his heart? It was shattered.

Nineteen

A Crown for the Wrong Man

The kingdom outside was falling. There was no denying it anymore. Whitecliff, once a beacon of power and pride, was now consumed by the flames of its own destruction. The city walls burned, the cries of the injured and the dying rising above the howling wind, carried into the castle on the waves of smoke. Yet, inside the throne room, there was no fire—just the cold chill of betrayal.

Kaela stood still, her breath coming in shallow bursts, her fingers clenching at her sides. The throne room that had once gleamed with riches, with promise, now felt like a tomb—a cold, hollow place where even the weight of the kingdom's legacy could not comfort her. Raelan stood before her, the crown heavy on his head, his hands trembling as he adjusted it, settling it into place.

It wasn't supposed to be like this. She had fought so hard, had believed so fiercely that there was something left in him— the Raelan she had loved. But the man before her now was unrecognizable. The rebellion had already claimed the streets outside, and now, the heart of Whitecliff had been taken over by the last vestiges of Raelan's ambition. The crown that he had once rejected was now placed firmly on his head, and with it, the final decision was made. The kingdom would fall, but not in the way Kaela had thought. It would fall under the rule of a man who was not meant to wear it.

Raelan turned to face her, his gaze vacant, lost. He looked like a puppet, bound by strings he could not cut. The fire in his eyes was gone. There was no rebellion left in him, no desire to rise above his station. There was only resignation.

Kaela didn't know what to say. The words were there, but they felt hollow in her mouth. She had spent years believing in him, hoping that one day he would be the man who would free them both from the darkness. Now, as she looked at him—really looked at him—she saw only a king who had traded his soul for a crown that wasn't meant for him.

"You've done it," she said, her voice thick with a mixture of anger and sorrow. "You've taken the crown. You've given in."

Raelan's expression flickered—just for a moment, like a candle flame threatened by the wind—but then it settled back into something darker, colder. "I didn't take it. It was given to me."

The words hung in the air, like a bitter confession, and Kaela realized in that instant that it didn't matter anymore. Raelan had never wanted to be king, but he had wanted to survive. And to survive, he had given everything up—the very thing that had made him who he was. The man who had dreamed of a better kingdom, of something worth fighting for, was gone. In his place stood a man who wore the crown, not because he had earned it, but because he had succumbed to it.

"Raelan," Kaela whispered, her voice breaking. "Why?"

He didn't answer her immediately. His gaze flickered toward the throne again, the weight of it seemingly sinking into his bones. For a long moment, he seemed lost, adrift in the sea of choices he had made. But when he finally spoke, his voice was as empty as the room around them.

"Because I thought it was the only way to save them," Raelan said, his voice soft, barely audible over the crackling of the distant fire. "I thought if I took the crown, I could protect Whitecliff. I thought if I wore it, I could make it better." He shook his head, his fingers running through his hair in frustration. "But I was wrong. I've destroyed everything. I've destroyed us."

Kaela took a step closer, her hands trembling at her sides. The weight of his words sank into her, but it wasn't enough to undo what had been done. The kingdom was lost, and with it, all the dreams they had once shared. Raelan had chosen this—he had chosen power over everything that had mattered.

"You didn't destroy us," Kaela said, her voice shaking with a quiet, fierce intensity. "You destroyed yourself. And now you're letting it happen to Whitecliff, too. This isn't about saving anyone, Raelan. This is about you—about your weakness."

Raelan flinched at her words, but there was no fire in his eyes, no anger in his heart. There was only the cold realization of what he had become, and the slow, inevitable surrender to the man he was now. The crown that sat on his head seemed to weigh heavier with each passing moment.

"Maybe you're right," Raelan said quietly. "Maybe this was always going to happen. Maybe I was never strong enough to make the choices I needed to."

Kaela's heart shattered, but there was no time to grieve. The rebellion was already inside the walls. Outside, the battle raged, the final stand of those who would see Whitecliff freed.

"Raelan," Kaela said, stepping forward, her voice desperate. "This doesn't have to be the end. You can still stop this. You can still change your mind. You can still fight for Whitecliff. Fight for what you said you believed in."

His eyes met hers, and for the briefest of moments, Kaela saw the man she had loved—the man who had been willing to risk everything for something better. But then it was gone, replaced by the hollow emptiness of a king who had already given up.

"I can't," Raelan said softly. "I've made my choice. I've already destroyed everything."

Kaela's eyes burned with unshed tears. She wanted to scream, wanted to force him to see the truth, to make him understand that this wasn't just about the kingdom. This was about them. But she couldn't. She couldn't force him to see the truth when he had already convinced himself that there was no hope left.

Just as the silence between them stretched, as if the weight of the kingdom's fate was settling in their hearts, the door to the throne room burst open.

It was Roderick.

Kaela's breath caught in her throat. She had known, deep down, that this moment would come—the final confrontation. Roderick had always been a shadow, lurking in the background, pulling the strings. And now, with the rebellion at the gates and the crown within reach, he had come to claim his place in this final act.

Raelan turned slowly, his gaze flickering between Kaela and the man who had once been his closest ally. But there was no warmth in his eyes now. There was only resignation.

"Roderick," Kaela said, her voice cold with the bitterness of everything she had come to realize. "I thought you were gone."

Roderick smiled, his expression dark and filled with malice. "Gone? I've never been gone, Kaela. I've just been waiting."

Raelan's gaze shifted to Roderick, his face drawn with exhaustion. "What do you want?"

Roderick's smile grew wider, his eyes gleaming with satisfaction. "I want what's mine," he said, stepping closer to the throne. "I want Whitecliff. And I'm not leaving here without it."

Kaela's heart raced. This was it. This was the moment she had feared—the moment where everything came crashing down. Raelan was already broken, but Roderick? Roderick had always wanted more. He had always wanted everything, and now, with the throne within reach, he would stop at nothing to claim it.

"You think you can just take the throne?" Kaela said, her voice rising. "You think you can just walk in here and claim it like it's your birthright?"

Roderick's laughter was sharp and cold, a sound that sent a chill down Kaela's spine. "I don't think, Kaela. I know. Raelan never wanted this. He's too weak. He's never been strong enough to lead this kingdom. But I am."

Raelan stood frozen, his eyes fixed on the two of them, the weight of his decision settling deeper into his bones. "No," he said softly. "This is wrong. I should have fought harder. I should have—"

But it was too late.

Roderick's hand shot out, grabbing Raelan by the collar and slamming him against the stone pillar. "You've lost, Raelan," Roderick hissed. "You've lost everything. Now, it's time for me to take what was always mine."

Kaela's heart stopped. She lunged forward, but before she could reach them, Roderick pushed Raelan aside, sending him stumbling toward the throne. Raelan hit the floor with a loud thud, his breath coming in ragged gasps.

Kaela's hands trembled as she reached for her dagger, but Roderick was already standing before the throne, his hands reaching for the crown.

"No!" Kaela shouted, but it was too late.

Roderick placed the crown on his head, and in that moment, Whitecliff was truly lost.

Raelan lay on the floor, his eyes empty as he looked at the man who had just taken everything from him. The throne, the kingdom, the legacy—they were all gone.

And as Kaela stared at the crown resting on Roderick's head, she realized with a sickening certainty that the worst had already come to pass.

Whitecliff was no longer a kingdom. It was a prison. And Roderick was its warden.

Her heart shattered in that moment, the pieces falling like dust at her feet. It wasn't just the kingdom that had fallen. It was everything she had ever believed in.

Twenty

A Thief's Farewell

T he night air was colder than usual, sharp against Kaela's skin as she stepped into the shadows beneath the towering walls of the castle. Whitecliff was still burning, the city's heart now reduced to embers and smoke, and yet, here she stood, on the precipice of something final. The crown, the kingdom, the rebellion—it was all in the past now. What was left of it anyway. What was left of her.

The weight of the moment pressed down on her chest, the last of her breath caught between the unspeakable decision she had made. She had walked away from him. Walked away from Raelan.

And it felt like she had ripped a piece of herself out in the process.

But it was necessary. She had seen it—she had seen the man who had once burned with rebellion, with hope, now nothing more than a puppet under his father's control. Under Roderick's control. She had seen the crown sit heavy on his head like a noose, strangling the life out of the man she had loved, and she had made her choice. She had to leave. She had to.

And so, she found herself here, in the dead of night, alone in the shadow of the kingdom she had once believed in. Alone with nothing but the echoes of her decisions and the pain of a heart she knew would never heal.

Her hands trembled as she gripped the leather satchel hanging at her side, the familiar weight of the tools she'd carried for so long feeling like a distant memory. She wasn't a thief anymore. She couldn't be. There was no more stealing to be done. There was nothing left to take.

Kaela paused as she neared the castle's outer gate, the moonlight bathing the path ahead in a pale glow. The city's turmoil was fading into the distance, but the sounds of battle still lingered in her mind. She had left him behind, left the castle, left the fight—left everything. Her heart was shattered, but it was the only way to survive.

A sound behind her made her stop, her senses sharp despite the cold. The rustle of cloth against the stone, the soft scrape of boots on the cobbled path—it was faint, but unmistakable.

She turned sharply, hand reaching for the dagger at her side, ready to defend herself, but she froze when she saw the figure standing in the shadows. A figure she knew all too well.

"Roderick," she whispered, her voice tinged with a mixture of disbelief and resignation.

Roderick stepped forward from the dark, his silhouette familiar in the dim light. His smile was small but knowing, and it sent a chill crawling up her spine.

"You're leaving, then?" he asked, his voice smooth, like the calm before a storm. "I should have known you'd try to slip away."

Kaela's pulse quickened, but she forced herself to remain still. "What do you want, Roderick?"

He cocked his head to the side, studying her with a detached curiosity. "I want what I've always wanted, Kaela. I want to know why you're so determined to destroy yourself."

She clenched her jaw, her fingers tightening on the hilt of her dagger. "I'm not destroying anything. I'm leaving. It's the only choice I have left."

Roderick took another step forward, his gaze never leaving her. "You think leaving will solve anything?" he asked softly, as though he were toying with her. "You think you can walk away from all of this—from him—and just disappear into the night?"

Kaela's heart skipped at the mention of Raelan's name. Her throat tightened, and for a moment, she thought she might break down right then and there. But she didn't. She couldn't.

She had made her choice.

"I don't want to talk about him," Kaela said, her voice steady but cold. "I've made my decision, Roderick. It's done."

Roderick smiled again, that same knowing smile, and took another step toward her. "It's never done, Kaela. Not when it comes to Raelan. Not when it comes to you."

She backed up, her steps slow but deliberate, her fingers never leaving the dagger at her side. "What are you trying to say?" she asked, her voice sharp, wary.

"I'm trying to say that you can't run from what's been set in motion," Roderick replied, his voice softer now, almost coaxing. "You think you can walk away and disappear into the shadows like you always have, but this time, it's different. He's different. Raelan is broken, Kaela. And you—you—have always been his weakness."

Kaela's heart thudded painfully in her chest. She hadn't expected Roderick to see through her so easily. Of course, he knew. He had always known her too well, always understood the dark corners of her heart, the places she had never shown anyone. But she had never realized just how much control he truly had over them both.

"I'm not his weakness," she said, her voice tight with the effort it took to keep her composure. "I'm not anyone's weakness."

Roderick's eyes darkened, and for a moment, Kaela saw something far more dangerous in him—a flicker of malice, of anger that he had carefully buried beneath the veneer of charm and manipulation. He stepped closer again, and she felt the weight of his presence pressing in on her, forcing her to confront the reality she had been avoiding.

"You think you're leaving to save yourself," he said, his voice low and menacing. "But you're not. You're leaving because you know he can't be saved. You know he's already lost to the crown. And so are you."

Kaela's breath caught in her throat. She couldn't breathe. The weight of his words hung in the air between them, suffocating her, drowning her. She wanted to deny it. She wanted to say that she was leaving for herself, that she was walking away to save whatever was left of her soul. But Roderick was right. She wasn't leaving to save herself. She was leaving because there was nothing left to save. Raelan had already given up. And she couldn't be part of that anymore.

"You're wrong," she whispered, her voice breaking. "I'm leaving because I have to."

Roderick didn't say anything. He just watched her with those cold, calculating eyes, his gaze never wavering. And then, in a flash, he moved forward, his hand gripping her arm with a force that made her gasp.

"No," he said, his voice sharp. "You don't get to walk away. Not now. Not when you've already broken everything."

Kaela struggled against his grip, but his hold was firm, unyielding. The dagger at her side felt suddenly too far away, too useless to help her. She had always been quick, but Roderick had always been quicker. And in this moment, she realized that she was more trapped than she had ever been before.

"Let me go," she hissed, her heart pounding in her chest. "You don't control me, Roderick."

He chuckled darkly, a sound that sent a shiver down her spine. "You still think you can control this, don't you?" he asked, his grip tightening on her arm, forcing her to look up at him. "You can't, Kaela. You never could. Raelan's fate was sealed the moment he took that crown. And yours?" His gaze softened, but there was no warmth in it. "Yours was sealed the moment you fell in love with him."

Kaela's stomach twisted painfully. She wanted to lash out. She wanted to scream at him, to make him feel the rage that had been building inside her ever since she had seen the man Raelan had become. But she didn't. She couldn't. There was no strength left in her for that.

"I never wanted any of this," Kaela whispered, her voice barely audible. "I just wanted to believe in him. I wanted to believe in something better."

Roderick's expression shifted, his grip loosening just slightly, but his eyes remained cold. "You still think there's something better?" he asked. "Something worth saving?"

Kaela's heart shattered at the question, the finality in his words pressing down on her, forcing her to confront the truth she had been avoiding. Raelan was lost. He had given everything for a crown that wasn't his to claim. And now, she was walking away from him, not because she didn't love him, but because there was nothing left to love.

"I don't know," she said, her voice breaking. "I don't know anymore."

For a long moment, Roderick said nothing. He just stared at her, his gaze unreadable, before finally releasing her arm. "Then go," he said quietly, his tone almost gentle. "Go. But don't think you can leave this behind. You're still part of it, Kaela. You always will be."

She turned away, her heart heavy with the weight of his words. She couldn't look back, not now. She couldn't afford to.

But as she walked away from him, from everything, she felt the last thread of hope snap inside her. Raelan was lost. The kingdom was lost. And she had nothing left but the pieces of a shattered heart.

A thief had taken her farewell, and now, she had nothing but the remnants of a dream that had never been hers to begin with.